EARTH'S MIND

ESSAYS IN

Earth's

NATIVE LITERATURE

Mind

Roger Dunsmore

University of
New Mexico Press
Albuquerque

To my students
Especially to those of American Indian ancestry,
who have so often been my teachers.

© 1997 by Roger Dunsmore
First edition. All rights reserved.

ISBN-13: 978-0-8263-1798-8

Library of Congress Cataloging-in-Publication Data

Dunsmore, Roger, 1938–
Earth's mind: essays in native literature /
Roger Dunsmore.—1st ed.
p.   cm.
Includes bibliographical references and index.
ISBN 0-8263-1798-7 (pbk.)
1. Indians literature—North America—History and criticism.
2. American literature—Indian authors—History and criticism.
3. Indian philosophy—North America.
I. Title.   PM157.D85   1997
897—dc21   97-4872
CIP

Designed by Sue Niewiarowski

Contents

Foreword

When we stop and reflect on it for a moment, the vast body of literature on American Indians is designed to give us information. It may give us some fleeting sense of how it was to be an Indian, but rarely does it force us to think deeply about anything. Much of it is history, a good deal of it descriptive narrative about art, crafts, conditions, and problems, and today we have a bevy of new biographies which now threaten to become a genre in and of themselves.

Roger Dunsmore has lived among Indians for many decades and has taught at the college and reservation level and so he is not a summertime "experiencer" of Indians rushing back to the coast to crank out a first-hand (albeit briefly experienced) story about Indians. Rather he reflects on his years in the West, ponders the meaning of his memories, and produces a set of essays that asks us to consider whether we have learned anything or thought anything after our encounter with Indians. This offering is therefore a new turn of events in literature on Indians—the proposal to go where few people have gone, to paraphrase Star Trek—and to consider what various messages from Indians might actually mean.

Drawing on the works of Leslie Silko, Black Elk, Simon

Ortiz, meditating on the sayings of Chief Joseph and his high school students' logs, and connecting their thoughts with the insights of Laurens Van der Post, Goethe, J. Gleick, and Gary Snyder creates an intellectual/emotional blend that reaches out to the rest of our species even while bringing us toward our own centers. It is not enough, Dunsmore is saying, to read the thoughts of Indians. Our task is to take the ideas, bring them to our inner selves, make them our own, and then see if they have applicability in our lives and in the lives and values of the people around us.

What is it that we, as individuals and as societies, are to make of this strange kind of existence that we are condemned to experience? Does distinctive culture color our perceptions or do we respond to police killing a stray dog in universal ways that connect us with life as it struggles to confirm itself everywhere? Dunsmore gives his answer to these questions, ruminating over the connections that seem to bind our lives into particular pathways which, unfortunately, we identify only after we have moved through situations. Dunsmore does not try to *become* an Indian, only to find a meaningful life with insights gathered from his experiences with Indians.

We very much need reflective literature. A stock question in television and newspaper interviews is "What can we learn from Indians?" and regardless of the answers given, no clear direction ever seems to emerge that we can usefully employ in our own lives. Indeed, the relationship of Indians with the natural world has become so much a cliché that it no longer communicates anything except the need for petting zoos for urban children. The larger intimacy with the earth which makes petting unnecessary is addressed by Dunsmore in an important essay. He takes seriously the idea that mind (and/or spirit) really does manifest itself, at least in particular ways, in our relationship with the earth. Some tribes believed that the physical world was mind as fully manifested and Dunsmore moves to the brink of metaphysics before he pulls back and retains the idea for his own wisdom and understanding.

So we have thoughts — thought-provoking and engendering thoughts — reflections, meditations, and finally realizations. Most of all we have enjoyable literature.

— Vine Deloria, Jr.

Perhaps my greatest debt is to Nicholas Black Elk and John G. Neihardt for the quality of their collaboration on the creation of the text *Black Elk Speaks*. I first read it somewhere in the North Atlantic, on board a Yugoslavian freighter headed for Greece in the fall of 1966. I had just left my job as an English comp and humanities instructor at the University of Montana; the rubble of a first marriage; and my country, whose involvement in Viet Nam drove so many young people into voluntary exile. I remember feeling good about leaving on a ship with a giant red star painted on the stack. I didn't expect to come back.

Someone on board gave me a copy of *Black Elk Speaks* when they heard I was from Montana. I'd been reading an anthology of modern European poetry. All I remember is Miguel Hernandez's "Lullaby of the Onion." He was a goatherd sucked into the Spanish Civil War, dying of malnourishment and tuberculosis in a Franco prison in 1942. "Lullaby" was written from prison to his infant son who had nothing to eat but an onion:

I awoke from being a child:
Don't you awake!

My mouth is sad:
Laugh forever!
In your cradle
defend laughter
feather by feather.

Mostly I felt suspended between the two continents, between old and new worlds, somewhere at sea. During rough weather, at night, a couple of us would pick our way forward around the tractors and combines chained to the deck, lie on our backs in the bow and watch for shooting stars, or stare into the blobs of pale-green, watery luminescence plowed up by the ship.

I hadn't imagined that men like Black Elk were contemporaries of mine. I'd thought of them as belonging to a past that was both gone and inaccessible, especially to mid-western farm boys like me. But here they were, the purported words of a man from the deep human past in America, carrying the wisdom and pain of a 40,000-year-long hunter/gatherer tradition into my own time. And here I was, on my way to Greece. I thought if I could drink the same light that Homer and Sophocles and Socrates and Euripides had drunk, then maybe I could understand enough to live.

I saw some of that intense Greek light, especially how it ate away the faces of the marble lions lining the avenue from the sea to the dried-up, sacred lake surrounded by palms in Delos, ruined city of a ruined god, Apollo. The last lions in Greece were killed by 300 B.C., about the same time these stone ones, crouched, began roaring at the sky. Their eyes are smooth dishes of milky marble now, like the eyes of Athenian beggars eaten by the larva of a special fly that lays its eggs in the pupil.

But the light of Greece aside, and its darkness too, reading *Black Elk Speaks,* I knew something I hadn't known when the shoreline of this continent receded into the haze off the stern of the M/V Klek. I knew there was something for me to return to in North America. Something I could not name but which resided in the land and which had sustained the people of the land for millennia. Somewhere in the North Atlantic, suspended between worlds, I knew I could go home.

※

I'd like to thank two of my early teachers who have had a powerful and lasting influence: Philip Young of Penn State who presented the study of literature as if it were jazz improvisation on a grand scale, and who always seemed inspired. And Henry Bugbee at Penn State and the University of Montana whose experiential philosophy taught us "*the union existing between the mind and the whole of nature*" (p. 135). This collection of essays would not have been possible were it not for his work in the philosophy of religion.

I'm grateful to Gary Snyder for always being there along the way that is no way and for publishing the Black Elk essay early on. A University of Montana Small Research Grant in 1975 supported me while writing the Black Elk piece, and a University of Montana sabbatical in 1981 got me through a first, book-length draft that laid the foundation for this one.

A. LaVonne Brown Ruoff in 1983 at the University of Illinois, Chicago, and Larry Evers in 1987 at the University of Arizona in Tucson ably lead NEH Summer Seminars in American Indian Literature that stimulated and goaded me into the writing of many of these essays and gave me a sense that my work belonged to an emerging discipline. I'm grateful to Karl Kroeber of Columbia University for publishing three of the essays in the mid-80s in his journal, *Studies in American Indian Literature,* and to Vine Deloria, Jr., for including the Black Elk piece in his volume commemorating John Neihardt's one-hundredth birth date.

The year 1988–89 as Humanities Scholar In Residence at a large Indian high school on the Navajo Reservation gave a needed reality check to my work. I'm grateful to the Arizona Humanities Council and the Tuba City High School Boards for that opportunity (and to Felipe Molina for bringing the Deer Dancers to the school and for his encouragement on the clown piece).

A few long-term friends read substantial parts of these essays, gave astute comments, and believed in the project. I'm deeply in your debt: Margaret Kingsland, Eleanor Danesh (who also did most of the initial typing), Richard Conway, Ed Lahey, and Dexter Roberts. To Steve Osborne, for being there in Greece, and ever since, and for letting me live in the shack behind the house while I wrote on Black Elk. Many thanks.

I am especially grateful to Frances Vanderberg, Victor Charlo, Willy Brown, Buster Yellow Kidney, Merrill Yellow Kidney, Victor Masayesva, James Peshlakai, Leon Rattler, and Danny Vollin, Indian friends here in Montana and in Arizona whose shared lives and historical/cultural knowledge have greatly deepened what I might have accomplished on my own.

From those I've overlooked, I ask forbearance.

Lastly, to Nancy Neal, for teaching self-respect and for taking me into Indian country; and to Victorio, wherever you are, for teaching me to listen to the rocks.

Introduction

These essays are the track of a beginner's journey on the path of earth's mind. I wrote them over a seventeen-year period (1975–1992) in response to my teaching, first; classes of Indian students only, and then American Indian Literature in various humanities, wilderness, and environmental studies programs at the University of Montana. And one summer of teaching at the state prison in Deer Lodge.

There are seven reservations in Montana — the homelands for Salish, Kootenai, Blackfeet, Gros Ventre, Assiniboine, Sioux, Crow, Northern Cheyenne, Cree, and Chippewa peoples, as well as the landless band of Little Shell Cree and many Metis. The Indian communities in small cities here (like Missoula or Butte) are also made up of people from forty-some different tribal heritages. Here "the people" always are present, even when no one is recognizably Indian: people of mixed Anglo-Indian ancestry may look white, but carry a direct connection into the Indian world, often through grandparents who raised them.

Young Indian people began to show up more and more often in classes after my return to the university in 1968. This increase was a direct result of the establishment of an Indian studies program on this campus in 1969. Too often these students were not adequately prepared for the university, and the culture shock of moving from the reservation towns to the more cosmopolitan setting of Missoula was often difficult for them. James Todd and I, the two full-time humanities professors, went to Alonzo Spang, the new head of Indian Studies, in 1971 and asked how our program might assist Indian people trying to make their way in the university. He suggested a special section of Humanities exclusively for Indian students. Admittedly, at first it was more than a little daunting facing a roomful of Indian students from every reservation in Montana. I remember the irregular attendance patterns, the difficulties with written papers in English, and the mistrust that occasionally led to serious misunderstandings; but I also recall stunning displays of intelligence that came from angles of perception I hadn't imagined, and an intense Lakota man who, for a month, sat in a back corner laughing softly to himself and then disappeared across the bridge over the river one morning with his star blanket over his shoulder.

This influx of young Indian people into the university in the late 1960s, many of them struggling and the institution responding as if they were no different from other students, gave my interest in the literature an added stimulus. And the accumulated knowledge they carried in regard to the land was as necessary a gift as it was beautiful. It is important to point out, however, that Indian students are often confronted with intimidating situations in classrooms where they are expected to know and speak publicly about their traditions. As one young native student put it recently:

What I realized this afternoon is that I have never been alone in a class like this before. What I mean is, I have never been the only native in a class before. . . . I was never the sole representative for an entire nation of people. . . . I believe in my heart that I am a story-teller. But in this class, as I look into the faces of my classmates, I feel they want answers and I am afraid I may not be able to give them the answers they want. And that has been my underlying discomfort. The feeling of not being what they want." (Crawford, paper)

Nevertheless, Indian people in classes at the University of Montana have been remarkable, both in their willingness and in their ability, to teach from the context of their own respective heritages.

Those students who are at some cultural distance from their heritage, or who are Anglo, also respond deeply to these materials. Consider, for example, the Salish/Anglo man who looks like a younger version of his uncle, who runs a sweat up on the reservation: This young man had never sweated with his uncle, never hinted to the rest of the class that he was part Indian, and claimed to be from a very strict Christian family. But in his papers he wrote about his father, dead of alcoholism at thirty-five years, who always kept a thirty-inch iron bar under his car seat — his "nigger killer," he called it. "Niggers" was his term for white people. The young man had seen him beaten severely from the car window as a child by three white men outside a reservation bar. What I remember most about this student, though, was the intensity of light and energy in his eyes any time Indian subjects came up in our humanities class.

A young Blackfeet woman, responding in her journal to *One Day in the Life of Ivan Denisovich*, opened up a whole new angle of perception for me. Our class had been discussing Solzhenitsyn's description of Ivan's ability to maintain his basic human dignity while living in the dehumanizing conditions of a Siberian slave labor camp. Among other things, Ivan always took off his cap before eating; he kept a scrap of neatly folded cloth that he used as a napkin; he refused to eat certain foods given inmates — like fish eyes in the soup — on the basis of them being unfit for human consumption. The young Blackfeet woman wrote about the difficulty of defining "dignity" "simply because of the word 'human' attached." She described how the term has been misused:

It's sort of similar to (the phrase) "in the interest of progress." We had to do this and we had to do that "in the interest of progress." People have a tendency to fall back on something like "human dignity" when they've done something they're ashamed of. I think if you wanted to describe true dignity — it would have to be the dignity of wild animals. . . . it is human arrogance (firm belief that man is superior because of his power of reason) that causes us to attach the words "human" or "man" to admirable qualities. In any case, I see Ivan Denisovich as a man of dignity. Probably more so since he entered prison. He had compassion for his fellow prisoners and consideration for his wife. All of which was carefully hidden from prison guards and officials, but never off his mind. (Reeves, Journal)

This student was obviously thinking in a way that was different from how the other students were thinking, how I was thinking, and how anyone around me, especially other teachers, said they were thinking. I wondered why she wrote that a description of "true" dignity would be the dignity of wild animals. Her statement that our arrogance causes us to attach the word "human" to admirable qualities intrigued me. From where else but the human could admirable qualities come? She knew clearly about the abuse of language, an abuse often entailing the use of high-sounding words to mask shame. And she knew about prison what most of us would never learn — that a person's dignity might actually increase there. She viewed the over-culture with skepticism; she valued a certain intimacy and protectiveness that were highly conscious as well as instinctive, and she valued her personal connection to the wild.

In my comments at the end of her journal entry, I asked, "Can you give a description of a specific animal in its dignity?" I fully expected some standard response like "a bull elk on a ridge in front of a sunset." Next day I received the following entry in her journal:

I seen the cops catch a wild dog that had strayed too close to Browning & had killed a couple dogs. We stayed on the edge of town & right across the street was a big ditch. On the other side of that was the campgrounds. Anyway, they took the dog on the other side and tied him up. They then came back about thirty yards. I was about seven and counted the shots. Thirteen times they shot him. The first time he let out a big yelp, then he seemed to know they weren't going to stop so he'd just grunt a little every time another bullet would hit. After they finished shooting at him, they drug him away. He wasn't dead. His back was broke about three places and his legs, everything. He didn't seem to have a will, but I felt then that he was still proud.

That was the first lesson I got in human dignity. I often thought about it afterward. (It was the first time I'd seen anything get killed outside insects.) I wondered why they didn't put a gun to his head and pull the trigger once, letting him die in dignity & leaving themselves some, too. (Reeves, Journal)

This student let me know with great clarity why she had difficulty with the word "human" attached to the word "dignity." I could discern a whole history behind her perceptions—the history of 180 years of cultural contact between Blackfeet and Anglos. A history that would also help us to understand these two men, policemen shooting to pieces a wild dog. And there is a whole heritage behind these perceptions, too, a heritage that recognizes the immense value contained in all forms of life, including rocks and grasses and wild dogs; a heritage where knowledge of the necessity for remaining closely in touch with the animal powers, the star beings, was reinforced by the disasters of disease, starvation, and corruption that Blackfeet people had endured with the coming of the Anglo world.

Hers was not the only example of student work of this kind. While less frequent than I had expected, such examples popped up often enough. One young man wrote about his grandmother: How she would take scraps of bread and go out on the prairie near a colony of gophers and talk "Indian" to them, "very softly," until they gathered around her. She would scold them if they fought over the bread scraps. Later, he would walk out onto the prairie and sit "for hours" among the gopher mounds. He remembered lying on his stomach in front of a hole and having a big gopher come "within inches" of him. He tried to remember his grandmother's words then, but couldn't. Even his father couldn't remember them. Later still, when as a teenager he went gopher hunting for the first time and shot one, his grandmother, gone then, returned, bringing pain to his heart. I also remember a young Yakima, responding to a discussion of reciprocity, who described his family's giveaway following the killing of his first deer at nine or ten years of age. The giveaway was to celebrate the life of the deer. Not his prowess in taking it, he explained, but the giving of the deer's life to the boy and, through him, to the people. Nevertheless, he recalled being shocked when his own rifle was given away to a boy from a family without the ability to buy one. It would be many months, a year perhaps, before he could acquire another. That Yakima student's response clarified the obligations we all incur by the sheer need to eat. Taken as a whole, such examples testify that much of the Indian perspective has survived the maelstrom we call "the settling of the West," and that the context supplied by native students is critical when teaching the literature and history of their cultures.

And I hope that readers will see the essays in this volume as the path in the development of an idea — the idea that "mind" is much, much more than the human brain; the idea that our minds are merely one form of the expression of mind in the world; the idea that there is mind in things, the idea that the soundest minds, like Black Elk's, like Chief Joseph's, or like Matsuo Basho's, have a clear and deep understanding of the ways in which their own minds are linked with, say, the mind of the earth. This idea is very old and widespread, one prevalent in some major religions like Hinduism, in some Greek philosophy, and at the core of almost all aboriginal thought. The same idea is also fostered by many contemporary poets, philosophers, and Oriental writers. I'm thinking, for instance, of Gary Snyder's *Earth House Hold*. In the third part of a section entitled "Dharma Queries," a section largely concerned with Oriental traditions and with the survival within them of "archaic Nature-and-Man traditions," we find the following passage:

> Long hair is to accept, go through the powers of nature. Such are the Shaivite yogins . . . I knew a Wasco Indian logger (a faller) who quit logging (Warm Springs Camp A) and sold his chainsaw because he couldn't stand hearing the trees scream as he cut into them.
>
> He apprenticed himself to an old shaman and let his hair grow long. (p. 133)

For me, the point Snyder makes about the importance of long hair connecting one to the powers of nature, of this fact in Oriental and Indian traditions, is less powerful than his example. The example became the point, became that which sparked my mind and stuck like a burr in the memory. He couldn't stand hearing the trees scream as he cut into them with his chainsaw. It was not just the different way of thinking about trees that was startling. This was a different way of experiencing them. The Wasco logger experienced trees as living beings of a kind I understood only slightly, if at all. The first time I read that passage, it became a direction for me. I did not know, exactly, what it meant to open my consciousness in the direction of the trees, and I did not know how to move in that direction; I simply knew it was the direction necessary for me to go, but blindly, like those Greek beggars with devoured eyes.

One of the mainstays of my teaching in these years (1968–1988) was the seventeenth-century Japanese haiku master Matsuo Basho's *Narrow Road To The Far North*. A friend recited his favorite haiku:

Do not follow
in the footsteps
of the ancient ones.

Seek what they sought.

I presented this haiku as an example of how a traditional society also maintained flexibility. The students, rightfully, began asking: What, in fact, did these "ancient ones" of Basho seek? Or, were there clues, at least, as to what Basho had thought they sought? Near the beginning of Basho's *The Records of a Travel-Worn Satchel,* I found what I thought was a clear answer:

all who have achieved real excellence in any art, possess one thing in common, that is, a mind to obey nature, to be one with nature, throughout the four seasons of the year. Whatever such a mind sees is a flower, whatever such a mind dreams of is the moon. It is only a barbarous mind that sees other than the flower, merely an animal mind that dreams of other than the moon. The first lesson for the artist is, therefore, to learn how to overcome such barbarism and animality, to follow nature, to be one with nature. (p. 71)

The phrase "a mind to obey nature" crystallized much of what I'd encountered in American Indian materials and linked with Chief Joseph's statement, "The earth and myself are of one mind." What was this mind of which both Basho and Joseph spoke so succinctly? And how might one foster it in this time, this place? Had we, collectively and for centuries, been out of our minds? Was the Wasco Indian logger responding to or with this mind when he heard the trees scream? What, really, is the nature of mind?

On looking more carefully into the passage, however, I was confused by Basho's attitude toward animals. Why is it an "animal mind" that dreams of other than the moon? What had happened by the last half of the seventeenth century in Japan to make it possible for such a master as Basho to use animals as an example of "barbarism?" Basho's attitude seemed much less "obedient" to nature than that to which I'd grown accustomed from American Indians who respected animals as persons of another kind with their own gifts, as beings who might bestow on a fasting person with a sincere heart a power, an identity, a helper spirit. Whatever the case, it appeared that the Japanese by the time of Basho, wonderful as he was, had decisively broken the elemental link with the animal kingdom that native people here still maintain.

Yet, Basho was a help. He spoke of linkage with objects, of "poetry" emerging "of its own accord . . . when you have plunged deep enough into the object to see something like a hidden glimmering there" (Basho, 33). It was unclear to me what that "hidden glimmering" was. Might it be what others called the object's "spirit" or "mind"? Was it like what the Wasco logger heard as he cut into trees with a power saw? And how did one go about "plunging into" objects? What if the object did not wish to be "plunged into"? Did objects have any choice in the matter? Did they ever take it upon themselves to "plunge into" humans? Was "plunging into" objects having "a mind to obey nature"? Was the translation from Japanese into English misleading? "Plunging into" seemed more aggressive than hearing the trees scream. Certainly it was more aggressive than walking out onto the prairie with a few scraps of bread and a gentle Indian voice, or lying on your stomach, peering into a gopher hole.

Although Basho was helpful, his ideas seemed like those of a person speaking from a condition of radical separation from objects. He reminded me of the English Romantics seeing "eternity in a grain of sand" and being accused of the "pathetic fallacy," of imposing their own thoughts and feelings onto objects and then thinking that the objects themselves actually contained those thoughts and feelings. At their best, I imagined, the Romantics must have glimpsed that "hidden glimmering" in objects and yet failed to do justice to it after so many centuries of cultural separation. The marvel is that they saw that "hidden glimmering" at all, and tried to give voice/mind to it. I found them to be neither "pathetic" nor "fallacious."

Basho also tells us:

Go to the pine if you want to learn about the pine, or to the bamboo if you want to learn about the bamboo. And in doing so, you must leave your subjective preoccupation with yourself. Otherwise you impose yourself on the object and do not learn. (Basho, 33)

The European Romantics intuited that "hidden glimmering," but without traditions, disciplines, and rituals for leaving their "subjective preoccupations" behind. Nevertheless, they re-opened that door into the "mind" in things, making it possible for us to hear Basho and the Wasco logger—the whole Native tradition of respect for other life-forms—now.

I found other clues. Martin Heidigger in his essay "The Thing" writes about how the old German word "thing" contained a sense of their power *to thing* (things "thinging") and how this thinging power of a thing gathered other things to it (Heidigger, 176–78). Meister Eckhart, that fourteenth-century forbearer of Heidigger, says, in a fragment on things, "One bursts through creatures when he lets go of things he has loved" (Eckhart, 233). How might "bursting through creatures" be similar to "plunging into things"? Is the "giving up" of which Eckhart speaks like the "leaving of the self" of Basho? All these ideas strained toward what seemed to be lived out with a grace and ease in American Indian lives and materials. The Wasco Indian logger wasn't involved in dense, Germanic philosophical language, nor in highly refined Japanese haiku aesthetics, and anyone who thought he was committing the "pathetic fallacy" hadn't spent much time either with Indians or trees. What I found in the American Indian literature and students, hammered upon as their world has been these past centuries, was the continuance of a mind/heart that was both aware of its necessary linkage to mind in all its manifestations, and that contained disciplines, ritual structures, and ceremonies for generating and sustaining that mind capacity.

Recently, on the Nez Perce Reservation in Idaho, I asked around about the original Nez Perce word that would have been in Chief Joseph's mind when he made his famous statement: "The earth and myself are of one mind." I was told that there was no word in the Nez Perce language that meant mind—not any word that dealt with it as a separate entity. I thought of my beginning Chinese class — of the character '心' which, we were told, means heart/mind. The students didn't get it. "Isn't there a separate character for heart?" No. There was only this '心', this heart/mind character. I recalled Dorothy Lee's *Freedom and Culture*. In it she describes how Indian societies, like the Wintu of Northern California, assume different mental-linguistic structures than we do. For example, a key aspect of Wintu mental/linguistic pattern is a strong tendency not to fragment or separate parts from a whole. "Dog ail I" is Lee's rendering of how Wintus would say what we translate as "my dog is sick" (Lee, 132).

It is clear from this example that when we render "Dog ail I" into standard English we fracture and dismiss the Wintu world. We translate out of Wintu — way out — and into our own world view. We dissolve the whole quality of the relationship between dog and speaker and reconstitute it along separated and possessive lines. And I don't think that my language here — "the quality of the relationship between dog and speaker" — is accurate. There appears to be no "between" in the Wintu. There probably isn't a "relationship" that has a "quality" either. If we take seriously this difference in the way the world is constelled in other cultures, then what language of ours is adequate to describe what is going on in the Wintu world? One is reminded of how many times one has heard Indian people say, "If you really want to know us, to know our culture, our world, then you'll have to learn our language. The important things just don't translate." In the phrase "Dog ail I" the connection seems to be what is important. The "dog" and the "I" are bound together by the ailment, and much more. The bond is what is real, what matters. The ailment is shared — the existence of each participates in the other to the point that separate existence is not the essential factor.

Leslie Silko, in her novel *Ceremony*, describes this perspective of connection through the boy Tayo's understanding of his "auntie" who is so rigidly Catholic and so affronted by the mixed-blood offspring of her younger sister gone "bad":

> Only Tayo could hear it, like fingernails scratching across bare rock, her terror at being trapped in one of the oldest ways.

> An old sensitivity had descended in her, surviving thousands of years from the oldest time, when the people shared a single clan name and they told each other who they were; they recounted the actions and words each of their clan had taken, and would take; from before they were born and long after they died, the people shared the same consciousness. . . . ,". (Silko, p. 70)

This capacity to share one consciousness, to feel what the others are feeling in the chest and the belly goes far beyond the family and the clan. It extends to every aspect of the environment within which the people live, to the rocks and the winds. Such a perspective rests, I believe, on the pervasive experience and concept of the primal value of relatedness. To be successfully human, both individually and communally, is "to plunge purposefully deeper into the relatedness of all things," as Dorothy Lee writes in her essay "Responsibility Among the Dakota" (Lee, 61).

Perhaps Basho sought a memory of such relatedness in his admonition to "plunge into" objects? Certainly the Wasco logger is on his way to this mind/world. Many of our European ancestors also intuited it. As the old Celts liked to say, "Where human memory ran out then the memory of animals, plants, and rocks was available to be drawn upon" (Mathews, p. 108).

I offer this collection in the hopes that it may do its part —
"to reconcile the people with the stones."

No Boundaries

Two things hooked me when I first read this novel a decade or so ago: the description of the Gallup slum child left on a barroom floor while his mother worked as a prostitute, and the immense value and place accorded to the green bottle flies in the Laguna world. Of the first I thought, at last someone is going to tell the truth of the down side of Indian life, is not going to mask or avoid that. Of the second, the way even a creature as "dirty" and seemingly insignificant as a fly has its proper place in the scheme of the world, and is explicitly honored in one of the old stories — how thoroughly the whole world is perceived and valued. Even the flies. Everything else I have to say about this novel should be taken in the light of these two things.

Early in Leslie Silko's rich and closely woven story, *Ceremony*, there is a moment of seeing in which the so-called "normal" categories of space, time, and racism are absent. Tayo, the half-white/half-Laguna Indian protagonist is in the army, World War II, the Philippines. His sergeant tells them "to kill all the Japanese soldiers lined up in front of the cave with their hands on their heads," prisoners of war. Tayo can't do it. Sweat is stinging his eyes and his vision is unclear. In that instant he sees. He sees across thousands of miles of space, he sees across thousands of years of time, he sees across the barrier of the color of one's skin: he sees his old Uncle Josiah from back home at Laguna standing there with his hands over his head as if "he were about to smile at Tayo." The other soldiers fire, and he watches his uncle fall, and he knows it is Josiah. They shake him. They try to get him to stop crying, they force medicine into his mouth, they force him to look into the face of the dead Japanese soldier "and that was when Tayo started screaming because it wasn't a Jap, it was Josiah, eyes shrinking back into the skull and all their shining black light glazed over by death" (Silko, p. 7).

They have convenient names, labels, for his condition such as battle fatigue and hallucinations. Next day, they act as if nothing has happened, and Rocky, his cousin, reasons it out with him; shows him that it is impossible that he saw Uncle Josiah there, but Tayo only shivers,

> because all the facts, all the reasons, made no difference anymore; he could hear Rocky's words, and he could follow the logic of what Rocky said, but he could not feel anything except a swelling in his belly, a great, swollen grief that was pushing into his throat. (Silko, p. 8)

And so he vomits and vomits throughout the first half of the novel, until "their medicine drained memory out of his thin arms and replaced it with a twilight cloud behind his eyes" (Silko, p. 15).

What is going on here? Does Tayo see Uncle Josiah standing there among the Japanese prisoners being gunned down or not? What and/or how is he seeing? How could the facts and the logic and the reasoning of his cousin and the sergeant be wrong? Who is insane?

Tayo will make a long journey in this novel. It will be the journey from the psychiatric ward of a Veterans' Administration hospital where he has become invisible — because he believed the world of facts and logic and reasoning of Rocky and the sergeant was the true world and that he was only insane — to the kiva, the underground — ceremonial chamber of the elders of his people, where older, deeper ways of seeing are kept and honored, where he comes to the full understanding that "he was not crazy; he had never been crazy. He had only seen and heard the world as it always was: no boundaries, only transitions through all distances and time" (Silko, p. 258).

This perception that the world as it always is contains "no boundaries, only transitions through all distances and time," (or "that boundaries are all lies," in the words of another Indian woman writer, Linda Hogan) is one of the centers of this novel, and of American Indian experience. It is the belief in the reality of these boundary-lies that permits what Silko calls the "witchery" to perpetuate such crimes as the murdering of the Japanese prisoners of war and the creation of designs of "monstrous slaughter" from "the gray stone streaked with powdery yellow uranium, bright and alive as pollen" (Silko, p. 258), or the dumping of toxic wastes on impoverished nations, both inside the United States and abroad.

Strangely, Auntie, one of the most harshly drawn characters in the book, is also one in whom this sense of "no boundaries" is deep. Tayo comes to understand that her intense sense of shame, which translates into a powerful desire for social acceptance, comes from a "terror at being trapped in one of the oldest ways" (Silko, p. 70). Auntie feels her personal identity or self as tribal —

an old sensitivity had descended in her, surviving thousands of years from the oldest times, when the people shared a single consciousness, the ability to feel what the others [in her clan] were feeling in the belly and chest. . . . When little sister started drinking wine and riding in cars with white men and Mexicans . . . the Catholic priest shook his finger at the drunkenness and lust, but the people felt something deeper; in losing her they were losing part of themselves. . . . what happened to the girl did not happen to her alone, it happened to all of them. (Silko, p. 71)

Here the boundaries between individuals that we in the Euro-American society take for granted simply are not present. Auntie is connected to her little sister, to her shame, in a direct way that terrifies her. What happened to her sister, happened to her. That is the meaning of being a member of a tribal clan, according to Silko, to belong to a people in this way—to share a single consciousness. Tayo not only understands this in his aunt, he expresses the same way of experiencing the world when he sees the drunks in Gallup, New Mexico:

All of them slouched down against the dirty walls of the bars along Highway 66, their eyes staring at the ground as if they had forgotten the sun in the sky; or maybe that was the way they dreamed for wine, looking for it somewhere in the mud on the sidewalk. This is us too, I was thinking to myself. These people crouching outside bars like cold flies stuck to the wall. (Silko, p. 112)

This is us too . . . This connection of individuals to each other in a shared consciousness that will reach out to include all aspects of the local world, even to the grasshoppers and constellations, is a primary source for the experience that all boundaries are lies.

Another figure embodying this ability to move across boundaries is Night Swan, the old Mexican cantina dancer with eyes like a cat, with whom Josiah has his long affair during the drought. That woman, like water behind her sky-blue door, in her blue sheets and blue silk dress, with her green eyes, presides over the first half of the novel like spring rain, as

Ts'eh, Sunrise Woman, presides over the second half of the novel. These two women are different expressions, one secular, one sacred, of the same energy — the renewing life-energy that Tayo must link with, release in himself, in order to be healed, to take part in the larger, renewing cycles that sustain the people and the land, too.

(Tayo's mother, Laura, also represents this power to renew, even though she is a victim of the deadly attraction of the over-culture. Auntie, in describing her to Tayo, says:

> I stood on that sandrock, above the big curve in the river and there she was, coming down the trail on the other side. Right as the sun came up, she walked under the big cottonwood tree, and I could see her clearly: she had no clothes on. Nothing. She was completely naked except for her high-heel shoes. She dropped her purse under that tree. . . . It was empty except for a lipstick. (Silko, p. 73)

The power of her beauty and innocence and newness — her ability to maintain her connection to the world even in a life of prostitution and alcoholism, unites her to Night Swan. It is the moment of sunrise. It is the big curve in the river. She is naked, except for her high-heeled shoes. She walks under the big cottonwood tree. All the life-elements are here. And the immense vulnerability of native people to industrialized societies.)

To return to Night Swan, what we know of her is that she is a dancer, that that was all that was important to her. Dance, motion, those motions through which human beings get outside themselves, become some other, or vice versa. "I remember every time I have danced," she says, and recounts the story of an old lover. He tries to leave her because "his desire for her had uncovered something which had been hiding inside him, something with wings that could fly, escape the gravity of the church, the town, his mother, his wife. So he wanted to kill it, to crush the skull into the feathers and snap the bones of the wings . . . 'We will run you out of town,'" he says. That night, "she danced, spinning her body, pulling her thighs and hips into tight, sudden motions, bending, sweeping, veering, and lunging—whirling until she was the bull and at the same time the killer, holding out her full skirts like a cape" (Silko, p. 89). The men in the bar pull back, the guitar player finally lays down his instrument and holds his head in his hands; she dances on. She feels the floor boards begin to flex and glisten, she feels something breaking under her feet, the heels of her "dancing shoes sinking into something crushed dark until the balance and smoothness were restored once again to the dance floor" (Silko, p. 90). Her lover's wife comes into the bar screaming—he has been trampled to death by his own horses in the dark. Night Swan has danced out through the flexing boards, out into the horses, trampling this frightened lover who would have her run out of town to keep his own respectable life. It is an ancient image of bringing down the boundaries, dancers imitating the animals they are about to hunt—to establish an identity with them, to make the hunt successful. Or dancing into a trance state to open healing powers—to see the sickness inside a child or dying woman— to draw the sickness out. It is the dance way out beyond the limits of the horizon that Night Swan embodies—and hands on now to her granddaughters. And then she tells Josiah why she stopped in Laguna: "I rode the bus this far. I saw the mountain, and I liked the view from here. She nodded in the direction of the mountain, Tse-pi'na, the woman veiled in clouds" (Silko, p. 91).

This mountain, Mount Taylor, Tse-pi'na, Laguna's sacred mountain, is a dusty, dry blue color, where Ts'eh lives at the base, Ts'eh who calls herself "a Montano"; it is to this sacred mountain that Tayo is drawn also and where he finds the connections to the old/new patterns that both he and the people need. It is the spotted cattle who lead Tayo to the mountain, those "descendants of generations of desert cattle born in dry sand and scrubby mesquite who hunt water like desert antelope, unlike the weak, scarred, white-face Herefords who die off during drought" (Silko, p. 77). It is the spotted cattle who come from Night Swan's cousin, who treat fences — that clearest of clear expressions of the over-culture's commitment to boundaries — with utter disregard. It is of the spotted cattle Tayo dreams after going through the sand-painting ceremony with old Betonie. It is of the spotted cattle that he dreams after first making love with Ts'eh. They are like him — are him — mixed blood, partway between the wild desert antelope and the white-face Herefords. They are what Josiah will breed with the Hereford bull to get the best of both. They are what Tayo must become if he is to survive in this world, like Night Swan herself behind her blue door, beneath her great cottonwood which hides a part of the northeast sky at the top of her spiral staircase.

It is in relation to Mount Taylor and its lion that Silko makes her clearest expression of the reality of this world not being in the boundaries or fences we have constructed, but in the flow or motion of energy through the web of connections among things. After Tayo has cut a big hole through the fence the white ranchers have built, cutting through the lies inside himself, the lie that "only brown-skinned people were thieves," the lie that keeps white people from seeing that "theirs was a nation built on stolen land" (Silko, p. 199), he has a failure of nerve, an exhaustion, a fear that he's just been overcome momentarily by superstition, that Ts'eh is only in his head, and he collapses under a tree. It is precisely at this low point, this moment when he reaches the end of his own energy, his anger, and is vulnerable, that the mountain lion, the lion of the mountain, comes to him, just as it comes later when he is down in the hands of the cowboys, just as he sees Josiah among the Japanese prisoners when his eyes are stung with sweat:

His face was in the pine needles where he could smell all the tree, from roots deep in the damp earth to the moonlight blue branches, the highest tips swaying in the wind. The odors wrapped around him in a clear layer that sucked away the substance of his muscle and bone; his body became insubstantial, so that even if the fence riders came looking for him with their .30-30s loaded and cocked, they would see him only as a shadow under the tree.

The mountain lion came out from a grove of oak trees in the middle of the clearing. He did not walk or leap or run; his motions were like the shimmering of tall grass in the wind. . . . The eyes caught twin reflections of the moon; the glittering yellow light penetrated his chest and he inhaled suddenly. Relentless motion was the lion's greatest beauty, moving like mountain clouds with the wind, changing substance and color in rhythm with the contours of the mountain peaks: dark as lava rock, and suddenly as bright as a field of snow. When the mountain lion stopped in front of him, it was not hesitation, but a chance for the moonlight to catch up with him. Tayo got to his knees slowly and held out his hand.

"Mountain lion," he whispered, "mountain lion, becoming what you are with each breath, your substance changing with the earth and the sky." The mountain lion blinked his eyes; there was no fear. He gazed at him for another instant and then sniffed the southeast wind before he crossed the stream and disappeared into the trees, his outline lingering like yellow smoke, then suddenly gone. . . . He went into the clearing where the mountain lion had stood; he knelt and touched the footprints, tracing his finger around the delicate edges of dust the paw prints had made, deep round imprints, each toe a distinctive swirl. He kept his back to the wind and poured yellow pollen from Josiah's tobacco sack into the cup of his hand. He leaned close to the earth and sprinkled pinches of yellow pollen into the four footprints. Mountain lion, the hunter. Mountain lion, the hunter's helper. (Silko, pp. 204–5)

Silko's use of the word "beauty" in this passage cannot be emphasized enough: "Relentless motion was the lion's greatest beauty, moving like mountain clouds with the wind, changing substance and color in rhythm with the contours of the mountain peaks." The overriding tendency in the Euro-American culture would be to emphasize the power of the mountain lion—its teeth, muscles, and claws. Its ability to kill. And in hunting and killing lions, in having their skin on the floor or wall, mounted with open mouth to display the glistening fangs to the utmost, to identify one's own ego with the ferocious power of the lion that one has overcome with high-tech weapons and trained dogs. Silko understands the power of the lion, its abilities as a hunter, which is partly why she opens her statement of its beauty with the word "relentless." And why she has Ts'eh's consort, the old hunter that Tayo meets coming down off the mountain, wear a cap of mountain lion skin: The relationship of eater to what's eaten is the primal relationship. But the lion's "relentless motion," its power as a hunter, is part of something larger and more important—part of the great beauty which is the life-motion of this whirling earth, expressed at this moment in this story as the motion of wind through clouds drifting across the contours of the peaks of Mount Taylor, the woman veiled in clouds. Those winds, those clouds, carry the life-giving moisture to the fields and the lips and hearts of these dry-country, Pueblo farmers. The mountain is the source of their life, and to know the beauty in its cycles (of which the people are active participants in their own births, deaths, and marriages, with their hungers and ceremonies), is to know who they are, where they are, and what they must do to survive. To know it without the beauty is to strip it of its spirit, and to expose themselves to the fingers of the streets of Gallup. The sense of the great beauty of the motions of the mountain in her ongoing gestures underlies Silko's whole sense that there are no boundaries, only transitions. It is much more than the beauty of the lion of the mountain, its motion, that penetrates Tayo's chest at this point, that he sucks inside and to which he makes offerings of pollen. It is the full beauty of knowing that he, too, is a "child of the universe," that the boundaries between him and the lion, between him and what the lion eats, between him and the mountain, the clouds, the snow storm are illusory. His task, as always, will be to discover how to bring this knowledge down off the mountain and put it to work in his own life, in the life of his people, in their stories and land. But the point is that the whole experience pivots on beauty, ("the beauty and the strangeness of the earth," Black Elk calls it), the immense value of that. One thinks of the value placed on beauty in Navajo culture, where, according to Gary Witherspoon, a person's wealth is measured in the songs they in some sense "have," how a wealthy person is the one who has the power to generate, through story and song, an energy field of beauty reaching out into their family, clan, and land (Evers, pp. 99–100). Without beauty, the rest is mere technique, desire, tooth and claw.

When Tayo kneels over the footprints and traces the deep round imprints with his finger in the dust—those imprints, swirls of toe prints, are inside Tayo too, are the spiral staircase leading up to Night Swan's room. He makes his offering of yellow pollen from Josiah's tobacco sack, acknowledging his connection to these basic patterns and transitions. He has been prepared for this moment by the sand painting ceremony of old Betonie, led here by dreams and spotted cattle, and he will carry from this moment all he needs to survive, to recreate his life in accordance with the same rhythms and contours of mountain peaks and moon cycles as the lion. It was not

enough to have been through Betonie's healing ceremony—
Tayo must step within the ceremonial structure and patterns
of the world itself, finding the healing center there. The ceremony of Betonie is an expression of this, but not the source.

This ability to move in rhythm with the larger forces of
nature—mountain-storm-cloud-wind-moonlight-lion-beauty
—is the reality of the world as it always is, for Silko, moving
across all boundaries of time-space-fear-race-possessions.
Ts'eh, Sunrise Woman, embodies the gentler, feminine, side of
this power of the universe to regenerate and renew itself to
which Tayo finally comes:

> Sunrise!
> We come at sunrise
> to greet you.
> At sunrise.
> Father of the clouds
> you are beautiful
> at sunrise.
> Sunrise!
> (Silko, pp. 189–90)

He repeated the words as he remembered them, not sure if
they were the right ones, but feeling they were right, feeling
the instant of the dawn was an event which in a single moment
gathered all things together—the last stars, the mountain
tops, the clouds, and the winds—celebrating this coming. The
power of each day spilled over the hills in great silence. Sunrise. He ended the prayer with "Sunrise!" because he knew the
Dawn People began and ended all their words with "Sunrise."

> Sunrise,
> accept this offering,
> Sunrise.
> (Silko, p. 275)

There are many "small" places in this novel where Silko shows us the boundaries dissolving, being absent, or crossed:

—in the grasshopper wings buzzing in the weeds—the sound coming inside, making "his [Tayo's] backbone loose" (Silko, p. 229);

—in "a light yellow snake covered with bright copper spots like the wild flowers pulled loose and traveling" (Silko, p. 231);

—in the grasshoppers with "shiny thin legs with stripes of black and brown like beadwork making tiny intricate designs" (Silko, p. 164);

—in "the rain's children," frogs, "the color of the moss near the spring," popping up through the dry arroyo sands after a rainstorm, their backs spotted the color of wet sand (Silko, p. 99);

—in the plant Ts'eh digs, "containing the color of the sky after a summer rainstorm", which she will take and plant in a canyon where it hasn't rained in a while (Silko, p. 235);

—in the clay mortar of tumble-down walls washed away by rain, "the geometric patterns of rooms and kivas flowing into the white arroyo sand, where even the shards of pottery were rolled to pebbles, all their colors and designs soaked back into the earth" (Silko, p. 241);

—in the south-facing yellow sand rock cliff, alive with the lavender clay paint, the pregnant she-elk "startled forever across the curve of cliff rock, ears flung back to catch a sound behind her." "A'moo'ooh! A'moo'ooh! You are so beautiful! You carry all that life! A'moo'ooh! With you, the cliff comes alive" (Silko, p. 241).

Finally, in the cottonwood trees rooted deep in hidden waters, in the sky—

He [Tayo] smelled the waxy dark green leaves, and remembered climbing the big cottonwood trees along the river and plucking heavy hanging bunches of cottonwood berries that grew on the female trees late in the summer. . . . The smell of the crushed leaves had been exciting then because the cottonwood berries were ammunition to use against the other boys from the village, who tucked their shirttails into their jeans and filled the inside of their shirts with cottonwood berries until they had pendulous bellies. Then they ran, laughing and throwing handfuls of the green berries at one another.

The cottonwood trees had not lost their familiar feeling with him. They had always been there with the people, but they were much more than summer shade. After hundreds of years, when the great trees finally got too old and dry, the Ka't'sina carvers from the villages came searching for them to cut pieces of their soft dry wood to carve. (Silko, pp. 108–9)

When Tayo sees Uncle Josiah there among the Japanese soldiers, he sees truly—neither 30,000 years of time nor 10,000 miles of space nor vicious wartime race hatred can separate him from the true connections. As old Betonie tells him, "The Japanese. It isn't surprising you saw him with them. You saw who they were. Thirty thousand years ago they were not strangers" (Silko, p. 130).

What Silko gives us is a modern rendering, from the perspective of the native peoples of this continent, of a reality that is fundamentally different than the one on which Euro-American culture is built. We will not be sensitive to that other reality—to those transitions through many forms of life, to the beauty of this earth and sky across all boundaries and fences—as long as our attention is focused on the human characters in the novel. If we shift at least some of our attention onto the details of the natural world in which these humans find themselves, then Silko's meaning becomes clearer. Here, landscape is not merely setting or backdrop. The land where the Lagunas have lived for so many centuries is the people — has come into them — their bodies, minds, and spirits, and they have gone into it — so fully that they must be seen or understood together. The culture emanating from Europe understands this on some level — which is one reason why a policy of removal of Indian peoples from their land has been so prevalent in the history of "contact." To forcibly remove a people from their land is to sever them from the ground they are nourished by, from the ground they have become. The land is ancient, has given rise to many forms of life. Large and timeless forces are at work in giving the land its character, which changes always in accord with patterns. The people experience themselves as like the land, dependent on it and the forces expressing themselves through it. They are not separate from the land or set against it — they belong to it. They also live in a time when that belonging is threatened by a society of those who:

> . . . grow away from the earth
> . . . grow away from the sun
> . . . grow away from the plants and animals.
> They see no life
> When they look
> they see only objects.
> The world is a dead thing for them
> the trees and rivers are not alive
>
> . . .
> The deer and bear are objects
> They see no life.
>
> They will fear what they find
> They will fear the people
> They kill what they fear.
> (Silko, pp. 142–43)

This is not a book written against white people — Tayo is half white, Night Swan is green-eyed, Betonie is part Mexican and tells Tayo you don't write off all the whites, just like you don't trust all the Indians. But it is a book that understands that the power in much of the so-called dominant way of life emanating from Europe is a destructive one — one that separates and creates boundaries and turns away from the processes of nature — or tries to capture those processes for its own use. *Ceremony* describes another way of experiencing oneself and the world — one that allows the life of the mountain — and its lion, its beauty — to penetrate into the chest — and without fear, just as the green bottle fly is regarded as one of the original helping beings by the Lagunas. It is the deep linkage with all this that guides Tayo away from the trap Emo has set for him as he tortures Harley in a night scene of pure witchery. It is this which guides Silko to a different kind of ending to her book — one that doesn't promote the religion of violence so prevalent in the United States.

"The end of the story. They want to change it. They want it to end here, the way all their stories end, encircling slowly to choke the life away. The violence of the struggle excites them, and the killing soothes them. They have their stories about us — Indian people who are only marking time and waiting for the end. And they would end this story right here, with you fighting to your death alone in these hills. Doctors from the hospital and the BIA police come. Some of the old men from Laguna come too. They drive over there in their patrol cars." She pointed across the big arroyo to the place where the sandy wagon road was washed out. "They walk this way. The doctors have medicine to quiet you. The others bring guns. Emo has told them you are crazy, that you live in the cave here and you think you are a Jap soldier. They are all afraid of you." Her eyes filled with tears again. "They'll call to you. Friendly voices. If you come quietly, they will take you and lock you in the white walls of the hospital. But, if you don't go with them, they'll hunt you down, and take you any way they can. Because this is the only ending they understand." (Silko, p. 243)

But Tayo will end back in the kiva, where Laguna elders will listen as he tells the story, and question him about the direction she had come from and the color of her eyes, and guide his fast, while Pinkie and Leroy and Harley will die the violent death, and Emo will disappear into the cities of California.

But it is not nearly enough to see only the flaw in the thinking which is committed to boundaries. Aren't boundaries essential? Don't they establish necessary limits and set the terms for restraint? If there are no boundaries, then what is there to give form and structure to the world, to keep Tayo, and us, from drifting as white smoke in the V.A. hospital or seeping back into the dark earth again? Is the idea of "no boundaries" merely yet another expression of the desire to merge, a nostalgic longing for a golden age of oneness prior to separation from the mother or the emergence of societies from mythic into historical time? And if old Betonie doesn't exist in terms of boundaries, then what does he have to guide and structure his world, to keep it from formlessness and chaos?

Ceremony's answer to these questions is that there are patterns instead of boundaries, ancient, ongoing, organic patterns that exist on all levels, from the constellations to the grasshoppers, patterns that are interconnected and that are in our human makeup as well. These patterns are not walls or blockages; they are guides and enabling structures that reside in the textures and motions of life, but they have little or no market value and so are ignored by the over-culture, unless of course they are the patterns of uranium grains in the black rock.

It is no accident that Silko opens her novel with a reference to Thought-Woman, the spider, for this ancient being is the source and keeper of the primal patterns, expressed in her web as well as in the way a person's or people's thoughts weave together a story or a world. This pattern of the web is contrasted early on with Tayo's memory of the tangle of colored threads from old Grandma's sewing basket that have spilled out of his arms and that only snag and tangle tighter, like his memories, as he tries to rewind them. A spider's web is not a tangle, it is an ancient, effective pattern, and from such webs the people have learned the secret of weaving and pattern and being: the universe itself as a web of fragile yet potent interconnections of which we are but a single thread. The spiders know this, are this, and express it, spinning it out of their bodies, the net which is both home and trap, carrying within themselves, too, the poison that immobilizes their food. They are masters of life/masters of death — weaving it all together — keepers of the patterns of being, of non-being, old as air, old as rock:

But you know, grandson, this world is fragile.

The word he chose to express "fragile" was filled with the intricacies of a continuing process, and with a strength inherent in spider webs woven across paths through sand hills where early in the morning the sun becomes entangled in each filament of web. (Silko, p. 36)

The patterns of the stars, of Orion the hunter in the winter sky, the patterns of the mountains, of storms, of the designs on the legs of grasshoppers, the patterns in the old language, and in the rocks and plants, the pattern of the circle that the ants make when Ts'eh shakes them out of her shawl, that the snow makes when Tayo shakes it off the apricot tree onto the ground, these are a few of the patterns that sustain Tayo in the path of his own recovery, which also is the path of recovery for a people, and for their land.

Sucker

THE CIRCLE BACK (HOME)

Haboo, Vi Hilbert's fine collection of Lushootseed (coastal Salish) stories, includes "Journey to the Sky and Back Down to the Earth," a story by Charlie Anderson which expresses the surprising ways that pattern is present in the world, in Sucker's head. (Charlie Anderson is Vi Hilbert's father, which is one clear way of locating the meaning of "oral tradition.")

The Bitterroot Salish, the aboriginal people here in Western Montana, are the easternmost extension of Salish culture. They remembered their coastal heritage by partaking in the annual run of Pacific salmon up the west-slope-of-the-Rockies' rivers, especially the Lochsa, the Clearwater, and the Selway. They also followed the old Buffalo Road out onto the northern plains to hunt bison and mix it up with the Blackfeet, thus having the best of two worlds. Frances says she can understand the coastal people, though their dialect is different.

SUCKER
It was in the story
about the journey to the sky,
the one where the ripe salmon berries

grab the canoe maker and take him right up
just as he's reaching to pick them.

(Watch what you grab —
it might grab you,
like just-ripe berries
can grab in the guts.)

Everybody, animals, fish, birds,
went up in the sky to look for him,
that canoe maker who grabbed the salmon berries.
It was a stampede to get back down the sky ladder
after they found him.
It broke under the weight of all the big animals going
    first —
Black Bear, Grizzly Bear, Elk, and others,
and stranded a lot of people up there in the sky.

Sucker was an Indian doctor then.
He was stranded up there with the others.
"Don't be afraid," he told them,
and to get on his back.
Then he jumped.
He brought everyone back down from the sky.
But his head was not solid.

That's why he has bones of all shapes in him,
Eagle, Wolf, Fish, Hawk, Bluejay
and lots of others.
The old people could name every bone in Sucker's head,
and tell what animal it had come from
when he jumped down with them all on his back.
Sometimes
it's good to have a head

that isn't solid,
like Sucker.

You will find him rotting along the riverbanks
in our country:
no one will eat him,
too bony.
But you Lushootseed people,
you learned Sucker's secret,
you did:
the bones of all the animals,
a whole taxonomy
there in his soft head.

Earth's Mind

There are many holocausts (lit., burnt whole) in human history. Perhaps the most dramatic one today is the destruction of the rain forest in the Amazon Basin and in other parts of the tropics. It is a holocaust which destroys not only millions of Indian people, whose tribal names we will never know; it is a holocaust which is destroying the whole fabric of life — the plants, animals, insects, birds, fish, and the soil and air and waters of which they are an expression. The unimaginable richness of this environment makes its rapid annihilation all the more morally reprehensible, and all the more ecologically terroristic. It is estimated that one out of every six plants and animals on the planet live in the Amazon basin, and it is estimated that over a million species could be lost to extinction by the turn of this century. What makes the present holocaust in the tropical rain forests so numbing is that it is a naked revelation of the continuous holocaust against the land and against people of the land that has been a central feature of so-called civilization since before Sumer, in the interest of first agricultural and later industrial production. When we see the denuded hillsides and impoverished soils of the Eastern Mediterranean Basin, we see the primary costs of the building of the Greek and Roman fleets, with their attendant short-lived empires. And when we look at photographs of starving Indians in the "dust bowl" in this country, we see the primary cost of the destruction of the bison herds and the plowing of the prairie. We also understand that the acceleration of the rate of destruction of peoples and lands has risen exponentially in this century, in our own generation. All of this information is so well known as to have become almost commonplace, and hence, largely impotent. This information itself has become a commodity of "correct" liberal thinking.

Another truism we have inherited is that American Indians, and indeed native peoples everywhere, have a special relationship to land which is fundamentally different from the one fostered by societies such as ours. This essay explores that relationship of American Indians to land, as a response to the ten thousand-year-long continuous holocaust of which we are the inheritors and which finds its most dramatic expression today in the "burning whole" of the tropical rain forests. I wish to point to some of the sources out of which we might redirect our relationship to land. I take such ethical redirection to be imperative. I intend to indicate the nature and depth of the aberration to which our practices and policies of development have brought us, and the nature of the values necessary if we are to remain, at the very least, human.

The idea of earth's mind comes from a statement made by Chief Joseph, Hin-mah-too'-yah-lat-kekht, Thunder Traveling to Loftier Mountain Heights, in early May 1877, at the last council between the Nez Perce Indians and representatives of the United States government before the outbreak of what has come to be called the Nez Perce War. At issue was conflicting claims to the land. The government was there to "encourage" the Nez Perce to give up life on their ancestral homelands, including the Joseph band's beautiful Wallowa Valley, for survival on the Fort Lapwai reservation. Joseph, not a major spokesman at this council, made this statement:

The earth and myself are of one mind. The measure of the land and the measure of our bodies is the same. . . . If I thought you were sent by the Creator, I might be induced to think you had a right to dispose of me. Do not misunderstand me, but understand me fully with reference to my affection for the land. I never said the land was mine to do with as I chose. The one who has the right to dispose of it is the one who created it. I claim the right to live on my land and accord you the privilege to live on yours. (Humphrey, p. 105)

"The earth and myself are of one mind." This powerful statement coming to us across the barriers of language and time. It raises questions for us: How is it that the earth has mind? How is it that a man might share in that mind, or have "one mind" with the earth? What is that "one mind" which both Joseph and the earth are of? What does he mean by "mind" anyway? And what do we mean by "mind"? Translation difficulties aside, and these are no small matter, people like Joseph all over North and South America, both in the past and at this present time, speak from a highly-developed oral tradition of which they are masters. And they speak from within situations where absolutely everything that they know and love and are is at stake. It is not "romantic primitivism" or political rhetoric or poetical metaphor that we get from these speakers. It is the power and spirit and mystery of voice, primal voice, raised to its highest, finest level, in defense of ways of life that include not only oneself and one's people, but one's ancestors, the unborn, the land itself, and all the various forms of life through which the land expresses itself. It is voice in defense of all this, and much more that we do not begin to understand, at an historical moment when it all is about to come under the domination of a numerically and technologically superior people who, according to their own testimony, have lost their souls.

We think Joseph didn't really mean to say that the earth has mind. We think he talked in that way for effect—that it was just his way of indicating his deep connection to the earth. *"The earth and myself are of one mind."*

"Metaphorical" is our modern term that explains how it is that Joseph thought or spoke in this way. It is axiomatic that our explanations of how other people think are value-laden from our perspective and do violence to their experience. Our explanations are exhibitions of how we think other people think—not examples of other people's thinking. It is interesting to note that in most historical reconstructions of this last council of the Nez Perce and the United States government, Joseph's speech is omitted. Recently, I ran across a newer text in which it was included, but the opening sentence, "The earth and myself are of one mind," had been excised. Always, the tendency is to leave out and ignore that which we do not understand because it does not meet with our assumptions about what is real. The failure of white society to understand what it is that Indian peoples are saying to them lies in our inability to step back from our explanations of their statements and cultures and to listen to them in their own terms, in their lives as themselves. We don't understand "the earth and myself are of one mind" because for us the earth does not have mind. We have put great stock in the special province of human mind superiority over any and all other so-called manifestations of it.

All this leads us to consider just what do we mean by mind. What is mind? And who has it? John Swanton, an Alabama Creek Indian and anthropologist writing early in this century sheds some light on this experience of mind of which Joseph speaks:

The world and all it contained were the products of mind and bore everywhere the marks of mind. Matter was not something which had given birth to mind, but something which had formerly been mind. Something from which mind had been withdrawn, was quiescent, and out of which it might again be roused. This *mind* was visibly manifested in the so-called "living things" as plants, and . . . animals. . . . This might come to the surface at any time, and it did so particularly to the fasting warrior, the knower, and the doctor. Indeed, the importance of these last two types of people lay in their ability to penetrate to the human life [or mind, I would say] within the mineral, plant, and animal life of nature and to bring back from that experience knowledge of value in ordering the lives of their fellow human beings. . . . Mind was . . . recognized as everywhere of the same nature. (Swanton, p. 37)

Swanton is clear in his assertion that matter and mind are not separate, and in his statement of the ability of certain types of people to go within the matter of the world, to link there with the mind in things, and to bring back from that experience or journey "knowledge of value in ordering the lives of their fellow human beings." Mind is not, in this worldview, the special province of human beings, and human beings must not isolate themselves from the mind residing in "the mineral, plant, and animal life of nature," lest the human mind so isolated become impoverished and imbalanced. Species extinction, then, can be seen as a permanent form of impoverishment of our own consciousness possibilities; i.e., our very domination of other forms of life cuts us off from potential sources of renewal, redirection, and order. We are left at the mercy of our own self-created "orders."

This journey out into the mind that resides within the mineral, plant, and animal life of nature is actually a union of two journeys simultaneously. It is also a journey inward, for we have travelled through other life forms. Our oldest ancestors, back through mammals and reptiles and fish, are not absent. When Swanton speaks of that ability to go out into the mind in other forms of life, and when Joseph refers to sharing the mind of the earth, I think they also mean that they have journeyed to the spider, rock, and reptilian consciousness residing within themselves, within all of us. When we deny significance to other life forms, we deny significance to those parts of ourselves that were formed in our journey through them.

But we have not addressed the question of what we mean by mind. What is it, this mind that we place so much stock in, which Joseph shares with the earth, and which Swanton says resides within matter? Turning to Webster, we find that "mind" derives from the old Indo-European base word, mem-, "to think." And what does that mean, to think? Again from Webster, we find the Indo-European base word "tong," to thank. In the origins of our own culture, then, we discover the ancient connection between "think" and "thank." How are we to understand that linkage? Is true thinking thanking? Is thanking the primal form of thinking? Is the thinking which constitutes "mind" in our own origins the recognition of all that to which we are indebted for our bones, our skins, our tongues? To lose this primal linkage between thinking and thanking, between mind and thankfulness to all the powers of the world which engender and sustain us, is to usher in the culture of ingratitude.

American Indians have always been shocked by the sheer ingratitude that permeates the basic structure of Anglo society. It is why so many Indian terms for whites translate literally as "fat grabber" or "grabbing creature," "suyapi" in the local Salish dialect. It has been clear to them that this society has broken with the great cycles of reciprocity that connect us with all things, and all things with each other. Here is another Indian statement that gives powerful voice to that difference between the cultures:

> The Indian believes that he is a cannibal—all of his life he must eat his brothers and his sisters and deer and corn

which is the mother, and the fish, which is the brother. All our lives we must eat off them and be a cannibal, but when we die, then we can give back all that we have taken, and our body goes to feed the worms that feed the birds. And it feeds the roots of the trees and the grass so that the deer can eat it and the birds can nest in the tree. And we can give back. But today we can't even do this, you know. They poison our bodies and we can't bury our people. We have to be put in boxes to wait for some life, you know, that's going to be. . . . We are all going to rise up, which is so . . . different from the way we feel about our bodies and giving back. (Armstrong, p. 160)

The most dramatic part of this quote is the verbal jujitsu through which an abusive term, "cannibal," is turned into a positive term for kinship relationship to other forms of life, wherein both plants (corn) and animals (deer) are seen as relatives — brothers/sisters, mother. This sense of kinship to *all* other forms of life is world-wide among tribal peoples and expresses their experience of not being separate from or superior to the rest of creation. Other forms of life are potential teachers and sources of power, insight, vision. (The word "guru" in the Hindu tradition, for instance, originally meant any *thing* that is one's teacher.)

To return to our quotation, here one's body is not experienced as cut off from the bodies of worms, fish, corn, deer, trees, etc. Their bodies are taken inside ours and mingled there with us, become us, become our flesh and energy, and if there is to be a balance in the world, it is only appropriate (from the perspective of this speaker), that in the end our bodies be eaten too, taken inside the bodies of the worms, birds and mingled with the body of the land of which we are all part, "given back," as it says. We are them, they are us. And it is the soil with its processes of decay, ingestion, digestion that is the medium through which this endless transformation between one form of life and another goes on — eating, digesting, eliminating, dying, rotting, sprouting, these processes through which we exchange bodies with all that is around us — especially in hunter-gatherer and still in predominantly agricultural societies. If we are interrelated, as kin, to all other forms of life, then it is not possible to escape being a "cannibal." To acknowledge that is to accept the necessity (physically and morally) of giving back.

To return to the May 1877 council between the Nez Perce and the United States government: the person chosen by the Nez Perce to be their spokesman at the council was Toohoolhoolzote, the old dreamer prophet and medicine man, whose name means "sound, such as is made by striking any vibrant timber or metal with a hard substance." Toohoolhoolzote's words give us a sense of the importance of earth's body too. Toohoolhoolzote came to the council as spokesman for a nation that knew these were *their* lands, and to work out arrangements whereby the Nez Perce could live peacefully with the white settlers in their territory. General Howard chose to refer to him as a "crossgrained growler" and a "large, thick-necked, ugly, obstinate savage of the worst type" (Josephy, pp. 502–4), and placed him in the guardhouse at Fort Lapwai for one week during the council because he refused to give up his ancestral lands and go onto the reservation. (One can imagine the reaction of the U.S. military if Toohoolhoolzote's counterpart at this council, General Howard, the spokesman for his nation, had been taken by the Nez Perce and held for a week at the height of the negotiations between them.)

Toohoolhoolzote emphasized his connection to the land on which he lived with statements such as:

But I belong to the earth out of which I came. The earth is my mother (Josephy, p. 500).

You white people get together, measure the earth, and then divide it. . . . Part of the Indians gave up their land. I never did. *The earth is part of my body,* and I never gave up the earth [emphasis added]. (Josephy, p. 503)

Toohoolhoolzote extends the sense of the body that is in the cannibalism quote; he extends this beyond the linkage to other forms of life to the earth, land, soil itself. When we ask Joseph or Toohoolhoolzote or any people of the land to come onto the reservation, to give up their homeland, we ask them to give up a part of their own bodies. Their bodies have been formed out of that particular land — all the life through which it has expressed itself — and the soil of that land is rich with the bodies (and spirits) of all their ancestors who have gone down into it.

This explicit sense of the deep link between land and body is a common theme of Indian statesmen in their negotiations with the United States over the ceding of Indian lands. Curley, a Crow chief, says it in 1912 when he refuses to cede any more of his land to the federal government:

The soil you see is not ordinary soil — it is the dust of the blood, the flesh and the bones of our ancestors. We fought and bled and died to keep other Indians from taking it, and we fought and bled and died helping the whites. You will have to dig down through the surface before you can find nature's earth, as the upper portion is Crow.

The land as it is, is my blood and my dead; it is consecrated; and I do not want to give up any portion of it. (Deloria, pp. 166–167)

If one takes this experience of the land as literally a part of the bodies of indigenous peoples, then "relocation" of tribes becomes a literal means of destroying people — of severing them from the body of the land to which they are connected.

Frederick Turner, in his "Introduction" to *Geronimo, His Own Story*, puts it this way:

> The Chiricahua, indeed all the Apache, had the priceless inheritance of those who live so close to the natural world that they cannot ever forget that they are a part of it and it is a part of them.

Here is the approved Chiricahua method for the disposal of afterbirth: the mother wraps it up in the piece of cloth or blanket upon which she has knelt during labor and places it in the branches of a nearby fruit-bearing bush or tree. This is done because "the tree comes to life every year, and they want the life of this child to be renewed like the life in the tree." Before the bundle is placed in the tree, the midwife blesses it, saying "May the child live and grow up to see you bear fruit many times." Thereafter, that place is sacred to the child and to his parents. The child is told where he was born, and if possible, the parents take him back to that spot a few years later and roll him on the ground to the four directions. Even adults, when they chance to be once again in the area where they were born, will roll themselves to the cardinal points in symbolic communication with the great wheel that turns everything with it, "whose center is everywhere and whose circumference is nowhere." This is why Geronimo begins the story of his life with a careful description of the place of his birth and why, at the end of that story, he says that the Apache are dying because they have not been allowed to return to their homelands. To the Indian mind, a man's attachment to this homeland was not a romantic nostrum, but a vital necessity. A man sickened and eventually died — a whole people might die away — if cut off from the life-source of the land itself. And so Geronimo, that "bloodthirsty savage," ends his autobiography with a plea that has the unmistakable dignity of profound conviction: he asks the Great Father, Theodore Roosevelt, to return him and his people to their Arizona homeland. (Turner, pp. 32–33)

The simple details of ritually and literally connecting each person in the tribe to the particular place and life forms of his/her birth are described. It is not difficult to understand how, in such a cultural system, every bush and tree and rock, etc., becomes intimately known, and sacred. I would argue with Turner in his characterization of the Apache communication with the natural cycles as "symbolic," but that plea, to be returned to their ancestral homelands, is deep and pervasive among Indian peoples. It is an appeal to be returned to their ancestors, their lives, their bodies, their unborn, to the spirit that is them and their land. But that homeland to which they appeal to be allowed to return may be so altered by mining, logging, damming, or nuclear testing, that it is unlivable or unrecognizable. Or it may be coveted by the state for weapons testing, or toxic-waste dumping. One thinks of the situation of the western Shoshone of Nevada (hundreds of nuclear test explosions have been committed on their land) or the reports of children on Rongelap in the Marshall Islands, a U.S. "trust" territory, playing in the white fallout as if it were snow after the fifteen-megaton Bravo hydrogen bomb test of 1954. That bomb was one thousand times more powerful than the Hiroshima bomb, and the Marshallese had no warning as to the dangers of radiation.

Dwamish Chief Se-ah-th makes this experience of land clear in his 1855 council statement to Governor Stevens:[1]

You must teach your children that the ground beneath their feet is the ashes of our grandparents. So that they will respect the land, tell your children what we have taught our children, that the earth is our mother. Whatever befalls the earth befalls the children of the earth. If you spit upon the ground, you spit upon yourselves. Our dead never forget the beautiful world that gave them being.

Every part of this soil is sacred in the estimation of my people. Every hillside, every valley, every plain and grove, has been hallowed by some sad or happy event in days long vanished. The very dust upon which you now stand responds more lovingly to their footsteps than to yours, because it is rich with the blood of our ancestors and *our bare feet are conscious of the sympathetic touch* [emphasis added].

Difficulties of translation aside this is a remarkable statement, especially if we take him seriously as saying what he means rather than as engaging in political rhetoric or poetic metaphor. Some of these words we've heard so often, we are deaf to them: *Respect* — what does that mean? Literally, "to look again," and again. It carries with it the implication of blindness that is in so much a part of our seeing — look again if you are to see what and who really is there. This entails patience, tolerance for boredom, and a looking which penetrates. And note that he says the ground beneath your children's feet *is* the ashes of his grandparents. It is not like those ashes, it is those ashes. And then to the heart of it: "The very dust upon which you now stand *responds* . . ." This dust responds because it is the ashes of grandparents who remember the beauty of the world that gave them being. The opposite of remembering is not to forget — the opposite of "remember" is to *dis-member* — true remembering brings back together again and makes live, makes present, some old/new thing, some beauty of the world, that in our forgetting we dismember. (This, in fact, is what most distinguishes oral tradition from history. Oral traditions are not at all interested in the past. Instead, they are interested in memory, in the power of memory to selectively *presence*, to make present those experiences and events of one's ancestors that are most necessary to the ongoing life of the people. The accumulated mass of this remembered material is called a tradition, and it in no way is past. History's power lies in its ability to relegate things to the past, to distance them for analysis, to put them behind us. The oral tradition keeps in the present the gifts of our ancestors as a tradition.)

What Se-ah-th tells them is that the literal dust upon which they stand at the very moment of making their treaty, is alive dust, is the Dwamish grandparents, and is responsive. That is, that the touch between his bare feet and the literal dust on which they actually are standing at that moment is a mutually responsive touch in which the Dwamish feet are conscious of the lives, the spirits, of their ancestors present in the soil, and in which the soil itself is responsive to them, lovingly, as he says, and the Dwamish can *actually* feel that. Further, this ancestral memory in the very dust "re-members" the beauty of the world. Governor Stevens wants the land, but doesn't know the dust. The failure to take seriously on this kind of literal level the experiential reality of the American Indian represents our failure to understand both the Indian and this land, of which he is both a part and an expression.

What we appear to have, then, in this relationship between land and Indian people is an absence of what we in the Western tradition take to be fixed boundaries between ourselves and others, and between inside and outside worlds. That sort of fixed boundary simply is not present in these statements. Their bodies are the land and the land is their bodies, is their ancestors and their kin, the other life forms. And what they happen to be at this time in their bodies, is a momentary coalescence of being in the ongoing process of transformations from one form of life into another that is the life process of the land itself.

There's a similar understanding to this stated in a very few lines of poetry by Wallace Stevens, that insurance company executive poet who wrote these, probably, to keep himself sane. I quote them because one of the things I want to do is to indicate that that deep identity between land and people is not something that's been totally lost to the Euro-American tradition. But it's submerged. Here are Stevens' four lines:

> There are men of a valley
> who are that valley;
> the soul is composed
> of the external world.
> (Stevens, "Anecdotes of Men by the Thousands")

In the same sense as with our previous quotes, there's no fixed boundary between the deep within and the deep without. Stevens understands that we are the external world. In fact, that it is not possible to create a boundary between inner and outer worlds. The soul will reflect the world around it, which is why many people feel empty, scattered, or plastic, and why we have been fatally (for them) attracted to so-called primitive peoples; i.e., their souls are composed of the land, the world of nature that they are "of."

Another way in which this deep identity between land and human beings is expressed in a submerged way in the Euro-American culture lies in the etymologies of some of the central words in our language, as we saw in the connection between thinking and thanking. Take the word "human," for example. As a humanist, I was well aware that a standard post-Renaissance meaning of this word had to do with being in question — to be human meant to question, and to be a question to oneself. Who am I? What is human excellence? And as an environmentalist, I knew that the humanist tradition had been criticized as arrogant, patriarchal, anthropocentric, incestuous. I had read the philosophy of *Inhumanism* of the American poet Robinson Jeffers—fall in love outward: become the mountains, the stag drinking from the mountain stream, the stream itself. I'd also been deeply impressed by what I'd learned from Native Americans and their literatures about a humanity, a being human, that was built on a tremendous openness toward other forms of life, wherein the so-called "lower" forms of life were not "lower" at all, but had their own forms of power and beauty, and where to be a complete person, one had to open up to the spirit of some other form, to seek out a guiding vision, an identity and power for oneself and one's people as a gift from badger or sea lion or dragonfly or bitterroot or from a particular rock. I also knew that the name for the first man in the *biblical* creation story, Adam, meant earth, or red clay, so that in the early Hebrew oral tradition there was something similar to what is found in Native American cultures. And then I took a hard look at the old word *human*. Where did *it* come from? I went to my Webster's and looked it up and read the etymology and followed the connections. I found the Latin root word *humus*—soil, earth, like in "Adam" and Native American cultures, the ancient connection to the land that is our base. And I discovered another word from that same Latin root, humus; the word *humble*. So that in my own language the word "human" carried literally within itself the humus that we come from and return to it—it carried connection to the land, and the implication that to realize *that* meaning of being human, being humus, carried with it a fundamental humility. The so-called "arrogance of humanism" was only possible if the seed/crystal meaning of the word "human" itself had been forgotten, which it had. Human-humus-humble. Why had no one ever mentioned this in passing, let alone pointed it out?

When I put the human-humus-humble connection on the blackboard in my class, one of the students, a Crow man, said something in his own language, and explained to us that among his people they have a saying they say to someone who is having too high an opinion of her/himself. He translated it as "you're just dirt," and added, "it doesn't mean the same as if a white person said it, dirty; it's like that humus-human-humble on the board."

Humus
(for Willie)

When I put that old connection,
Latin, on the board —
human-humus-humble
you mutter something in Crow:

When somebody is bragging themselves up
we have a saying,
you're just dirt,
only it doesn't mean the same
as when white people say it — dirty.
It's like to be humble,
like that human, humus on the board.

You want to know if it's all right
to write about the river —

When we kill a deer
we cut it up into little pieces,
the parts that can't be eaten
and feed it to the river,
entrails, legs, horn.
An old man talks to the river
with the children:

I give to you today, deer,
who gave to me,

so that he may complete his journey.
Thank you.
We want the river to be strong.
We sing to it,
feed it deer meat.

The morning Elaine dies
you hear my voice break,
yours next to me
softer than fawn skin . . .

The earth is my body.
I never gave up the earth.
Creation's fire, in all things.
You're in bad shape
if you can't feel it:
(sun burst star fire)
and this row of black beads
spaced around the edge —
it's for the bad things.
They're part of it too.

Be humus Willie,
earth-man walking
this star-drenched plain.

Be humus Willie,
finish the journey,
rainbow river,
river of meat,
not for words,
soft as fawn skin.

Be humus Willie,

river of earth
walking
these stars.

This recovery of the understanding that to be human is to recognize we are humus, that the name of the first man, Adam, in our tradition means red clay, that true thinking is thanking and thanking truly is thinking—all these are a beginning, from within the white society, of a basis from which to understand Joseph and the other voices of American Indians as they express Earth's heart/body/mind.

NOTES

1. Rudolf Kaiser, in his article "Chief Seattle's Speech(es): American Origins and European Receptions," reprinted in Arnold Krupat's *Recovering the Word*, discusses all four versions of Seattle's speech.

Killing the Water

Wind from an Enemy Sky, D'Arcy McNickle's last book, published posthumously in 1978, is set among a fictional people, the Little Elk Indians, whose culture and place strongly resemble those of the Flathead Indians in western Montana, among whom McNickle grew up. He himself was not Flathead, but a mixed-blood Cree (French and Irish).[1]

Wind from an Enemy Sky is a rich book, as well it should be, for McNickle struggled more than thirty-five years to bring it into its published form. His letter to Dodd Mead in July of 1940 says of it:

> It weighs on my mind in a heavily unsettling manner. I am beginning to have nightmares over it. Ideas for other books keep coming to mind, but I fight them off. I can't work on anything else until I get this off my chest. . . . I do want you to understand I am desperately anxious to complete the manuscript and get it out of the way.

It seems clear from a look at the early versions of the manuscript — more than four hundred pages hand written in pencil — why he couldn't finish it. The early drafts end far too happily to be true to what he knew to be the reality of Indian experience, or for their fictional representatives, the "Little Elk" people: He had Feather Boy's medicine bundle safely returned to the Little Elk people; Bull, the hold-out, grateful to the agent for its return and happily plowing up the land as a potato farmer; Rafferty, the model agent, getting a field promotion from his bureau chief for his successful negotiation for Feather Boy's return; Smitty, the young, female anthropologist falling in love with Rafferty in the process. No wonder the book gave McNickle nightmares!

The book we now have is a far cry from this charming romance. It is a complex tragedy that presents the disastrous collision between the Little Elk people and their guardians-helpers-destroyers in all of its painful reality. For McNickle shows how the structure of the encounter is such that even the best people on both sides, with the best of intentions (and here I mean Bull on the Indian side and Rafferty on the white), not only are unable to keep the tragedy from occurring, but in their best efforts at a reconciliation, they actually help to precipitate it.

At the center of this tragic aspect of the story stands the sobering figure of Adam Pell. As Pell discovers that he has both killed the Indians' water through damming the river and destroyed their most powerful medicine bundle through collecting it and not caring for it, he is consumed by guilt. And what McNickle presents so tellingly at this point is that it is exactly this guilt that is one of the most deadly things members of the dominant society have turned onto Indian people. The preoccupation with absolving his guilt for killing the water and destroying the bundle blinds Pell. He becomes incapable of thinking of the Little Elks—who they are, what they may need or want—and can think only of some magnanimous gesture, some gift, that will make up for his destructions. McNickle tells us through Pell that there are some things that can't be made up for, such as killing the water and destroying by neglect the sacred medicine bundle heart of a people. These things are irreplaceable. No gift, no matter how valuable, will replace them. No amount of guilt will replace them. And McNickle makes clear that Pell is more than one man among many. He represents a tendency within the dominant society. McNickle, like most Indians, knows this tendency well; there is some of Adam Pell in most of us. *Wind from an Enemy Sky* is a mirror into which we are asked to look and look again.

But I do not wish now to write about that aspect of this fine novel. I want to write about "killing the water," McNickle's phrase for the old peoples' feeling about the building of a dam.[2] Kerr Dam itself was welcomed by the Flathead for the economic relief it bought during the Depression years.[3] McNickle's dam is not Kerr; it's set too far up in the mountains, but McNickle is uncanny in his instinct for the long-term issue here — the fate of the water. The phrase "killing the waters" first appears in the text on page 2:

In a time not long ago, he [Bull] would have seen a stream break clear from the foothill below him and swing in a slow curve westward to spill itself in a river — a river, they said, which pushed through the mountains until it opened itself to a great sea of water. He could see even from where he stood that the stream was dry. The gravels and sands of its course had the look of bleached bones. So it was true, what his kinsman had been telling him. They had killed the water.

I began to ask around about this phrase and about water. It seemed to me to contain the central insight of the novel. I asked members of the Flathead Culture Committee, Johnny Arlee and Ron Therriault, if there were any songs, stories, or ceremonies having to do with water, with the river. I knew from a Crow friend that they still prayed to the Big Horn River, even though the state had claimed it:

> When we kill a deer, we cut it up into little pieces, the parts that can't be eaten, and feed it to the river—entrails, legs, horn. An old man talks to the river with the children:

> I give to you today, deer,
> who gave to me,
> so that he may complete his journey
> Thank you.

> We want the river to be strong, we sing to it, feed it deer meat—tell it that we love it—old men and children. (Brown, oral communication)

"No, we never did that," the Salish said. "We're asking the old people now to tell us what water is — we need to know — to protect it. The state wants it. The old people just tell us, it's life, it's in everything. Don't abuse it."

I thought about McNickle's/Bull's phrase—killing the water"—all through the later summer and fall. And I began to ask—water—what is that? Tell me about water. There were many answers. A young man, an apprentice sweatlodge leader, said:

> You can find out for yourself, you know. All you have to do is go without it for four days. I'll guarantee that on the third day you'll know what water is, you'll have your paper. When your saliva turns to white paste and you try to spit out all the poisons your body is releasing. It's life. That's why the woman always brings it in the Sun Dance, in the peyote meeting, because she brings life, like water.

A Jewish friend told me about an African novel, *God's Bits of Wood*. A young girl is told a riddle by her grandfather: Water washes us, washes the plants and streets and air. Water washes everything. What washes water? She comes back to this puzzle. It weaves together her experience. Water washes us, washes everything. What washes water? He tells her the answer at the end of the book: Spirit washes water. "It's just something that stuck with me," my friend said. I looked, but the book wasn't in our library. Besides, it was African, my friend was Jewish. What did all this have to do with Bull's "killing the water" from a novel by a French-Cree-Irish mixed-blood from the Flathead Reservation in western Montana?

Killing the water. With all this and more in my head, I picked up my telephone two weeks ago. It was Frances, my Salish teacher, asking if I could join her for lunch. When we met, I told her I had been working on the McNickle book, thinking about his phrase, "killing the water," and that I had realized we don't know what water is. "What was the word you taught us for water?" I asked her. "Seh-Wil-qwa." I listened. "Seh-Wil-qwa." She gently repeated it after each attempt of mine. I remembered that someone had told Art, another beginning Salish student, "Talk like you've got a mouthful of spit." Seh-Wil-qwa. I asked her for the literal translation. What does it mean, literally, to an older Salish person? Her eyes widened; she sucked air into her open mouth, both hands up in front of her face. "It's too big, too much," she said. "You can't translate it into English. It's complicated."

I persisted. "Well, can't you just talk to me for a couple of hours and sort of fill in by describing all the parts of it that don't translate? I mean, there must be a way in a paragraph or two, a page or two, that will tell about all those things that don't translate."

"I will think about it," she said. "You know, the man who could have told you, and he'd talk about it, too, died last summer. I'd go by his house every day and there were lots of things I wanted to ask him. Old Enaes Pierre — he really knew these things. He had a water story he told many years ago — I can't remember it — at the winter jump dances. It had fish in it and coyote and rabbit, and wolverine. He was so small, I always wondered if he had a wolverine spirit in him — no one ever said." We sat in silence, a university cafeteria buzzing around us. Frances pointed to my tea cup: "You know," she said, "that water that made your tea . . . I wonder about all the places it's been before it got into your cup. How many times has it been around the world, in the ocean, the sky, going through all kinds of different bodies? All those places."

We visited some more and departed. Next morning, I woke up with these memories:

A late April day, drizzling rain, warm. Only two of us appear for Salish class at the Arlee center. There's an hour of daylight left. "Let's go dig bitterroot," she says. We pick up Bones, the stray dog she's been feeding at tribal housing, drive across Finley Creek, the railroad tracks, up past the "No Trespassing Without Tribal Permit" sign, under high-voltage transmission lines. There is a boulder on the side of the hill where a transplanted grizzly bear ate a farmer's pig last year. A saskatoon bush bearing white blossoms grows right out of this boulder.

We dig on the hilltop in the light rain until it's too dark to see. The steel, curved digging tool is shiny-wet. Her fingers strip the outer skin of the bitterroots; it slips off easy in the wet. The root shines pure white in the failing light, its own light, shining. She shows us where to look for its heart, small red seed tucked up inside the root crotch, plucked, dropped back on the rocky ground. "So there'll always be bitterroot," she says. Meadowlarks call back and forth across this hilltop. "Uhwa-Whee," she teaches us their name.

The hilltop is littered with automobile- to shack-sized boulders from the last glacier — ten thousand years. Huge icebergs float in the ancient glacial lake formed by an ice dam two hundred miles west of here, Idaho now, many times. It is 1,400 feet deep where Missoula is today—a huge inland sea. It drains in a matter of hours when the ice dam fails suddenly—cubic miles of water all at once—giant ripple marks thirty feet high make little hills across Camas Prairie for five miles. That was a dam! Not this concrete block set in the narrow gorge the Flathead River cut in the bedrock knob south of the lake.

Here on this hilltop we dig amid glacial boulders deposited when the icebergs melted after the big lake drained. Seh-Wil-qwa. The People are a part of this hilltop, these shining roots, these boulders, this old lake, the icebergs floating 1,400 feet above us, this bottom of the sea—all in the word, Seh-Wil-qwa, the big eyes and hands in front of the mouth.

The river began to cut its way through time in this valley two million years ago, after the long dry spell in which the valleys filled with thousands of feet of sand and gravel. The Big Draw northwest of this hilltop is the old valley of the river, filled with glacial debris now—the surface covered with beautifully braided stream beds—dry for ten thousand years.

What I begin to understand, here on this boulder-littered hilltop that also is the bottom of the sea, is what the river—water—actually is. It isn't merely that fluid ribbon shining in the valley. The river is this valley, this whole valley floor, all the mud and sand and gravel here, the waves and undulations of water still present in the rolling hills—rivers of soil laid down by water flowing for tens of thousands of years—Seh-Wil-qwa. We look out over the rolling farmland of this valley and see the water moving all this earth, carrying and carving it. And the Mission Mountains covered with April snow that is melting down into this valley, evaporating into this air: Mountain rock crumbles slowly, breaks down toward ocean, ocean floor after the valley. It is this flow of energy down from the mountain peaks as they give up their rock to earth, to plants, to animals, to flesh—it is this great movement of rock into flesh and back again that is the river; the beauty and magic of water.

Several months later I saw Frances again, after she had spent a whole morning with the food stamp people — "They ask questions even God doesn't ask!" She had fish in the freezer, but would like other things for Christmas, like fresh vegetables. She'd rather have a job.

She starts by saying, "You can't think water without fish being in there somewhere. It's even all mixed up together in the sounds. You know Missoula isn't an Indian word; we don't know where it came from. Our name for this place right here where Missoula is, is In-thla'-eye. It is the name for Bull Trout. There were always a lot of them in the river right here west of the canyon, until the ice came. We could always get fish here. I don't know why, maybe they spawned in here."

I think of the Salish annual migration, over Lolo Pass down into Idaho, the Clearwater River, to catch the salmon run just as the streams swollen by the spring thaws began to fall. Each band chose its own tributary to throw a weir across; the catch gathered into a large pile under the band leader's supervision, bearers going from lodge to lodge around the circle while he counted out loud the number of fish to be laid before each lodge. And I think about the big fishery at Kettle Falls, ruined by the dams.

They also migrated east, across the big divide, after the bison herds on the west slopes were hunted out in the early 1800s: the old buffalo road to the Missouri River country. This country is the farthest reach of the Arctic shed — air-water-weather — the old Missouri River channel into Hudson's Bay turned south by the last glacier, and filled with glacial till, but cleansing Arctic winds, teaching endurance, still bring the weather, seeds, the birds. They skirted Triple Divide Peak, too close to the Blackfeet, though the Kutenais know it well, sacred mountain from which the snow melt water flows to three oceans — Pacific, Arctic, Atlantic. Seh-Wil-qwa.

"Did anyone ever tell you or did you ever see written down anywhere the story of Bitterroot?" she asks.

Long ago, as the story goes, in what we now call the Bitterroot Valley, Flathead Indians were experiencing a famine. One old woman had no meat or fish to feed her children. All they had to eat were shoots of balsamroot, and even these were old and woody. Believing that her children were starving to death, she went down to the river early one morning to weep alone and sing a death song. The sun, rising above the eastern mountains, heard the woman singing. Taking pity on the old woman, the sun sent a guardian spirit in the form of a red bird to comfort her with food and beauty. The bird flew to the woman and spoke softly.

"A new plant will be formed," said the bird, "from your sorrowful tears which have fallen into the soil. Its flower will have the rose of my wing feathers and the white of your hair. It will have leaves close to the ground. Your people will eat the roots of this plant. Though it will be bitter from your sorrow, it will be good for them. When they see these flowers they will say, 'Here is the silver of our mother's hair upon the ground and the rose from the wings of the spirit bird. Our mother's tears of bitterness have given us food.'." (Hart, p. 47)

The last thing she said before taking the old hill home; "About killing the water. I have great hope. They can't do that, though they'll sure try. But it's arrogant to think they can do that. The water can get to places we'll never even know exist. No. They won't kill the water. It was here in the beginning. It will be here in the end. I have hope."

This then, I think, is a beginning of an understanding of that phrase — killing the water" — of what water might be to these people who are named for the bitter, sustaining root that came from the hunger-tears, the sun, and the spirit bird, who carry the glacier-cycles, the fish migrations, in their knowledge that the earth is rooted in water. At the last forum to protest the proposal to build more dams on this river, Bearhead Swaney said, "if the river is clean, the people are clean. Everyone remembers." Water washes us, washes everything. Spirit washes water. Seh-Wil-qwa.

With these things in mind, Bull's anger at the dam becomes much clearer. He learns that his anger is as useless as the rifle bullet he fires at the dam, even the sound of that shot swallowed up in the louder sound of the dam itself. And when one of his young men shoots a young man of the dam, it is not only a useless act, but brings down on Bull's band of Little Elks the full weight of institutional racism in the person of the sheriff and the judicial system. And so Bull waits. He waits for an opening in the solid wall of white dominance around him, not in the hope that the dam will be removed or the water allowed to come alive again. He waits for a road to be made, a road for the Little Elk people on into a future that will not be stripped of their particular ways of being a people in these mountains, with these waters and skies. It is the possibility of the return of the Feather Boy Bundle that offers to him this hope of regathering the people around their ancient heart energy. And it is just this story of the arousal of this hope in him that is so breathtakingly cruel. For not only has his brother been turned into a "successful" white farmer, and been coerced by the priest into giving away their bundle as an expression of his "modernism," but those who would restore it to the Little Elks, Rafferty and Pell, are hopelessly naive about the way empire always has conducted itself in regard to the cultural loot it has stolen, cajoled, coerced away from the peoples of the land it has come to dominate.

This precious bundle, so feared by the priest, so coveted by the museum, so necessary to the Little Elk people, lies in utter neglect and ruin, thrown away:

Adam tore his museum apart — and made the final discovery. The medicine bundle had effectively disappeared, although not absolutely. It had been tossed into a lumber room, still bearing its identification tag, along with broken furniture, battered steel cabinets, abandoned exhibits, including stuffed birds and animals too mangy to be refurbished. But someone had failed to take it out of inventory and it showed up as a registered item. The unending battle museums wage against rats, moths, organic decay, and an assortment of molds, mites, and enterprising worms had caught up with the medicine bundle. Mice had eaten their way through the buckskin covering and had bred and reared countless generations, each generation chewing away at the hide and the inner contents, whatever that might have been. The only remains consisted of a few pebbles and the shafts of some feathers. Other objects may have dropped out, but no one had bothered to gather them up in disposing of the bundle. What was left of the hide and binding thongs were tattered and profaned, devoid of holy mystery. (McNickle, pp. 209–210)

(In discussing the differences between urbanized peoples and peoples of the land, I recently made the standard distinction between being and having: urbanites needing to have in order to feel complete, people of the land exhibiting a sheer intensity to be that is the completeness of the land and its cycles expressing itself through them. A young graduate student in environmental studies modified this: It isn't the distinction between being and having, he said, but between being and getting. The fate of the Feather Boy Bundle precisely expresses this distinction — the need to get something which, once gotten, is immediately forgotten and allowed to perish through possession as the "getter" turns his/her attention to the next thing to be "gotten" in the endless, empty process of seeking being through having.)

The viciousness and cruelty emanating from this enthrall-ment with getting, wherein even responsible having is de-valued, is intensified by the blindness of those so enthralled. Pell tries hard to understand what the processes of so-called "civilization" have meant to the Little Elks. And he persists to the point of another discovery:

> With kindly hands, they led him through the jungle of the law: to John Marshall: By common accord, the nations of the world recognized the right of each to chew off what it could, and to keep what it could hold; to Vattel: The nation with superior skill could appropriate to its own use the domain of a less accomplished people. They even led him to the Christian Bible: Multiply, and make the earth bear fruit.
>
> These were not sentiments, these were principles of inter-national politics — and how was it that he, a businessman of the world, should be raising such questions? Indian lands had been taken because they would be put to a higher order of use, because they would contribute to the ad-vancement of a higher order of society — and the law had legitimized such taking. The law was in society and society was in the law. Could he imagine what it would be like otherwise? Whose law, whose society, were irrelevant and immaterial questions. (McNickle, p. 190)

But to no avail. Adam Pell can see the way the law institu-tionalized greed, but he cannot see Bull. He cannot see the world from the place where Bull is. Rafferty, through sharing *years* of his life with the life of the Little Elk people and with the life of the place of which they are a part, has begun to understand. His naivete is in regard to his own culture, in regard to the massiveness of its blindness, self-preoccupation, and greed. And what makes the ending of this stark novel even more tragically true is that it is The Boy, the Indian police-man — who has also begun to find his way back — who kills Bull at Rafferty's order, shouting "Brother! I have to do this!" as the bullet from his pistol hits Bull point-blank in the heart.

Kill the water. The water of life. Build the dam. That which holds back, that which diverts, that which harnesses so we can generate energy. The medicine bundle, Feather Boy, is another kind of generator, not made of concrete and armatures with vast windings of wire, but with even vaster windings of spirit. What we do to the living water out there coming down off the mountain, flowing through the land, we do to the living water inside ourselves, blood and spirit. This is axiomatic. "The soul is composed of the external world."[4] What to drink? What to wash in? What water for the plants, the animals, the fishes? The rain becomes acid. Bull could have told us. The tall grass prairie species, fifteen to twenty feet high (corn is a grass), made and kept their own moisture. They were in the way. They swallowed up whole wagon trains. And the tiny yellow blossoms of grass seed along the dirt roads. Feather Boy. In the belly of rats. In the pungent molds. Acid rain falling all over the world. Bull, Antoine, watching it all.

No meadowlarks sang, and the world fell apart.

(McNickle, p. 256)

Seh-Wil-qwa.

NOTES

1. His mother had been taken in by the Flatheads. Her father had fought with Louis Riel in his attempt to establish a Metis state in Canada, and her grandfather had built the big-wheeled Red River carts that took the Cree all over the Northern Plains.

2. I am indebted to Frances Vanderberg, Peh les ah weh, my Salish teacher and friend, for much of the material in this section.

3. *The Place of Falling Water,* a three-part film by Thompson Smith and Roy Big Crane, presents a powerful version of the Salish/Kootenai experience of the building of Kerr Dam.

4. Wallace Stevens.

Nicholas Black Elk

HOLY MAN IN HISTORY

When John G. Neihardt found him in 1930, Nicholas
Black Elk had been living forty years at the end of a dirt road
in a square house with weeds growing out of the roof — an old
man going blind and wondering about the great vision of his
youth:

> And now when I look upon my people in despair, I feel like
> crying and I wish my vision could have been given to a man
> more worthy. I wonder why it came to me, a pitiful old
> man who can do nothing. Men and women and children I
> have cured of sickness with the power the vision gave me;
> but my nation I could not help. (Neihardt, p. 184)

More than any other deed, the annihilation of Big Foot's
band near Wounded Knee Creek late in December of 1890
made clear just how thoroughly the whites intended to destroy Black Elk's nation. Wounded Knee was not simply be-
lated revenge for Custer's death[1]; it made clear that the Lakota
had no recourse either in the institutions of this world or in the
powers of the other world. The Ghost Dance, which precipi-
tated the Wounded Knee massacre was a manifestation of the

desperate hope that the bison would return and the world would finally right itself by a people who had little remaining except that hope. Wovoka, the Indian prophet of the Ghost Dance, had said that

> there was another world coming, just like a cloud. It would come in a whirlwind out of the west and would crush out everything on this world, which was old and dying. In that other world there was plenty of meat, just like old times; and in that world all the dead Indians were alive, and all the bison that had ever been killed were roaming around again. (Neihardt, p. 237)

The hope that the white people would disappear, the belief that the old world would be renewed in familiar terms: it was for the desperate expression of these hopes and beliefs that the Lakota were punished by the United States Army. But they were to be denied much more than their lands and religion and bison. The U.S. government wished to deny them the very memory of the old ways of life.

It took a while for the Lakota to realize how much they had lost, but this realization played a large part in the forty years of wondering at the end of the dead-end road to Nicholas Black Elk's cabin: 1890–1930 — 40 years when "little else but weather ever happened."

What does it mean to be one who has received a great vision to protect and renew the life of one's nation in this kind of time? How might one understand the ease with which it was all swept away, that which had seemed so real and so beautiful, that for which one had been made responsible? What could it possibly mean to be a man of vision in the midst of all that? Nicholas Black Elk felt he was only a pitiful old man who was too weak to use the mighty vision that was given to him — so he gave the vision away to John Neihardt, "to save his Great Vision for men." He believed in the vision after everything else was gone: somehow the vision must go on. Although he didn't understand how his vision and its power could be released in the world, still he insisted: "But if the vision was true and mighty, as I know, it is true and mighty yet; for such things are of the spirit, and it is in the darkness of their eyes that men get lost" (Neihardt, p. 2).

How are we to understand Black Elk? As a warrior and hunter, one of the last generation to experience the old way of life on the plains before the bison were gone? As a scout for the U.S. Army and a performing Indian in Buffalo Bill Cody's Wild West Circus at Madison Square Garden and in European arenas? Are we to take him as Hehaka Sapa, the shaman and visionary, and the last surviving Oglala to have received orally the sacred rites of his nation, those handed down to him by Elk Hand, the former "keeper of the pipe"? Or as Nicholas Black Elk who was so fervent a Catholic Catechist that for many years he went around trying to convert his fellow tribesmen and who, after the publication of *Black Elk Speaks,* is claimed to have "made in English and in Sioux formal statements of his Catholic faith, signing them before witnesses lest he should be regarded still as a Pagan"?[2]

When we consider Black Elk's many identities and roles it becomes clear that it is not nearly enough to take him only in his role as a Holy Man of the Oglala. That is a beautiful and moving story, but it avoids considering what sense, if any, he made out of the disastrous relations between his culture and the invading white culture. In fact, Black Elk, even as a Holy Man, a man of vision, was so changed by the historical terror he experienced that he ended up giving away to the whites that which was most sacred in his own life and in the life of the tribe. *But* it is just this survival amidst a radical cultural and personal dislocation that gives him his strength and makes him important to us. For if we take him as a paradigm of what it means to be a man of vision, he revises our expectation that the holy man arrives somewhere at the Truth, at a truth which is recognizable to him and to us. Instead, Black Elk is deeply involved in not knowing, and confronts the risk that when he gives his vision away it will be ignored, misunderstood, or misused.

It is clear that during his lifetime, few white people heard Black Elk's voice. *Black Elk Speaks* did not sell well; the first edition was remaindered, and the book went out of print quickly. In 1947, fifteen years later, another white man, Joseph Epes Brown, found Black Elk partly crippled, almost completely blind, dressed in poor, cast-off clothing, living in an old canvas wall tent on a Nebraska farm where his family was working as potato pickers; a far cry from the perfectly enlightened, sun-tanned gurus proclaiming Truth in the Astrodome.

His life story tells us, then, that it is not enough merely to have had a great vision. A great vision is only a beginning, a starting place or point of departure, not an end, not final.

As I lay here thinking of my vision, I could see it all again and feel the meaning with a part of me like a strange power glowing in my body; but when the part of me that talks would try to make words for the meaning, it would be like fog and get away from me.

I am sure now that I was then too young to understand it all, and that I only felt it. It was the pictures I remembered and the words that went with them; for nothing I have ever seen with my eyes was so clear and bright as what my vision showed me; and no words that I have ever heard with my ears were like the words I heard. I did not have to remember these things; they have remembered themselves all these years. It was as I grew older that the meanings came clearer and clearer out of the pictures and the words; and even now I know that more was shown to me than I can tell. (Neihardt, p. 49)

From Black Elk's reflection, we learn that a vision must be free to direct one's life. It must not be frozen into some static truth-form. It is equally clear that what is important is the quality of one's response to that vision. A person must find some understanding of it, of what is being asked of one by virtue of having received it. What matters is the whole process of attempting to live with, from, and in terms of one's vision; to try to realize it in history, in the concrete situation in which one finds oneself. And what makes that response so powerful in Black Elk's case is that this process takes place under the most trying historical circumstances conceivable. While with Cody's Wild West Show in New York, Black Elk remembered that "after a while I got used to being there, but I was like a man who never had a vision. I felt dead and my people seemed lost" (Neihardt, p.221). Later in Europe, he discovered that "all the time I was away from home across the big water, my power was gone, and I was like a dead man, moving around most of the time. I could hardly remember my vision, and when I did remember, it seemed like a dim dream" (Neihardt, p. 235). Having a great vision insures nothing at all, not even a clear memory of the vison itself.

The implications of this loss of the clarity and power of his vision means that we must look at Nicholas Black Elk's *whole life story* as his expression of what it means to be a man of vision, and not focus too narrowly on the vision experience itself.[3] We must look at the slow, life-long process of unfolding of the vision's deeper meaning as he struggled to obey and fulfill it in an utterly intractable historical situation.

The process begins early and quietly for Black Elk: he is four years old, out playing alone, and hears someone calling him. He thinks it is his mother calling, but no one is there. This happens more than once, and always makes him afraid, so he runs home. Such a gentle beginning. His fear is curious, though it must have seemed strange to a little boy, and he seems unprepared. One is reminded of Najagneg, the Eskimo shaman who told Rasmussen that the "Silam," the inhabitant or soul of the universe, is never seen; its voice alone is heard. "All we know is that it has a gentle voice like a woman, a voice so fine and gentle that even children cannot become afraid. What it says is *si la ersinarsinvdluge,* be not afraid of the universe" (Rasmussen). Some such voice comes to Black Elk, a voice like his mother's, yet he is frightened.

The next spring, when he is five and out with his first bow and arrows, made for him by his grandfather, he gets a clearer experience of this voice. He is about to shoot a kingbird when it speaks to him: "Behold, a sacred voice is calling you; all over the sky a sacred voice is calling" (Neihardt, p. 19). This intense experience of the natural world as speaking directly to him is among Black Elk's most vivid memories from the beginning of his conscious life. He did not need to go on a vision quest: the sacred powers of the universe made themselves known to him. One might say that Black Elk is one who is sought out by these powers. He does not seek them out: this fact is central to Black Elk's role as a holy man. He is still afraid; as a holy man, he will no longer belong to himself, but to his vision and to his nation through his vision. He says that he likes to think about this early experience, but is afraid to tell it. He is afraid the adults won't believe him, that they will think he is only crazy.

In the years after the kingbird speaks, voices come back now and then when Black Elk is alone, but he doesn't understand what they want of him, so he tries to forget them. But the summer he is nine,[4] as he is eating with Man Hip, the voices announce very clearly: "It is time; now they are calling you" (Neihardt, p. 21). The next day Black Elk becomes very sick with swollen arms, legs, and face. Two men from the clouds come to him in his vision and he gets up to follow them and takes a journey into the sky on a small cloud. To all outward appearances, the young Black Elk lies unconscious

for twelve days, and his parents ask a holy man named Whirlwind Chaser to cure him.

Those twelve days of apparent coma are filled with dramatic events for Black Elk. He is summoned to a council of the
Six Grandfathers: the powers of the earth and sky, and of the
west, the north, the east, and the south, the six powers of
the world. He is taken to "the high and lonely center of the
earth" so that he can see and understand. He is given the
power to make live, the power to destroy, the power to heal
the sick, the power to sustain his nation, the power to make
peace, and the power to understand. He is called "younger
brother" by the powers of the world, told that he is their relative, and that "all wings of the air shall come to you, and they
and the winds and the stars shall be like relatives." He is given
a view of four generations in the life of his nation, including
the generation that will go through cultural annihilation.

The vision also includes the whole sky full of horses. Black
Elk "makes over" a faded brownish-black horse who turns
out to be a big, shiny, black stallion, chief of all the horses,
who sings a song that fills the universe:

> so beautiful that nothing anywhere could keep from danc-
> ing . . . the leaves on the trees, the grasses on the hills and in
> the valleys, the waters in the creeks and in the rivers and the
> lakes, the four-legged and the two-legged and the wings of
> the air—all danced together to the music of the stallion's
> songs. (Neihardt, pp. 41–42).

In short, Black Elk receives a powerful vision of the true
community of all beings. He is shown his actual relationship
to everything, including the very powers of the world, and he
is given the power and responsibility to care for his own nation in the midst of what will be a terrible future. The vision is
all unsought, given to a nine-year-old boy whose initial re-

sponse is fear that if he tells anyone about it, they won't believe him, youngster that he is. Though he can feel the meaning of it "like a strange power glowing in my body," and old Whirlwind Chaser can "see a power like a light all through his body," the young Black Elk is afraid the people will think that he is crazy, so he hides from Whirlwind Chaser (Neihardt, pp. 48–50).

The experience of the vision leaves a lasting impression, and for twelve days following it, he wants to be alone and feels that he doesn't belong to his people. During this time, when he is out with the bow and arrows his grandfather made for him, he thinks about his vision and feels strange. He tries to forget about it by shooting a small bird sitting in a bush. Just as he is going to shoot, he feels strange again, remembering that "I was to be like a relative with birds," so he doesn't shoot it. Then he feels foolish about that, and so kills a green frog by a creek, but is upset immediately.

It is clear that he will never be the same again. He will not take his relationships to other creatures lightly. Still, by midsummer he manages to quit thinking about his vision and in the following years there is much to distract him. Bison hunting, storytelling, the movement of whites into Lakota country with Custer's discovery of gold in the Black Hills in 1874, a big Sun Dance, Crazy Horse's defeat of General Crook on the Rosebud, the defeat of Custer on the Little Big Horn, the murder of Crazy Horse and the band's flight into Canada: all these events occur in quick succession. The band finally returns to its own country in the spring of 1879, when Black Elk is sixteen.

During those eight years (1872–80) of trauma for the Lakota, Black Elk seems to forget his vision and the powers he has received from it. At times he does receive help in finding game and in horse racing. He has protection while fighting, premonitions that something terrible is about to happen, and always there is a continuing sense of other creatures as sacred. Although the vision is hidden from others and largely forgotten, it is there at critical moments supporting and reminding him. Yet as he sees his nation being torn apart by warfare and undermined by the lies of corrupted chiefs such as Spotted Tail, he wonders if maybe his vision was only a queer dream after all.

After Crazy Horse is murdered and Black Elk's family flees to Canada, the vision begins to press him more as the desperate circumstances of his people deepen. He begins to wonder when his "duty is to come." His description of his emotional confusion just prior to his first public revelation of his vision shows us the increasing tension he was experiencing:

A terrible time began for me then, and I could not tell anybody, not even my father and mother. I was afraid to see a cloud coming up; and whenever one did, I could hear the thunder begins calling to me: "Behold your Grandfathers! Make haste!" I could understand the birds when they sang, and they were always saying: "It is time! It is time!" The crows in the day and the coyotes at night all called and called to me: "It is time! It is time!"

Time to do what? I did not know. Whenever I awoke before daybreak and went out of the tepee because I was afraid of the stillness when everyone was sleeping, there were many low voices talking together in the east, and the daybreak star would sing this song in the silence:

"In a sacred manner you shall walk!
Your nation shall behold you!"

I could not get along with people now, and I would take my horse and go far out from camp alone and compare everything on earth and in the sky with my vision. Crows would see me and shout to each other as though they were making fun of me: "Behold him! Behold him!"

When the frosts began I was glad, because there would not be any more thunder storms for a long while, and I was more and more afraid of them all the time, for always there would be the voices crying: "Oo oohey! It is time! It is time!"

The fear was not so great all the while in the winter, but sometimes it was bad. Sometimes the crying of coyotes out in the cold made me so afraid that I would run out of one tepee into another, and I would do this until I was worn out and fell asleep. I wondered if maybe I was only crazy; and my father and mother worried a great deal about me. (Neihardt, pp. 163–64)

Finally, his parents asked an old holy man, Black Road, to try to cure him. Black Elk's fear compelled him to tell the old man the visions, experiences, and turmoil that he had been carrying inside himself for eight years. "You must do your duty and perform this vision for your people upon earth," Black Road told him and added that if he failed to do his duty, something very bad would happen to him.

From this account, it is clear that to be a man of vision is, first of all, to be a man of duty. And the first duty to one's vision is to share it, not simply with an elder holy man, but also with one's people. To share the vision will release a person, and will also release the power of the vision into the world, into the life of the people. The very first act of letting go, of sharing, will eventually take the man of vision beyond his own culture. Not to share this vision, to contain within oneself all that one has received, is to turn the vision against oneself and to rob one's people of its benefits.

And so Black Road and another elder named Bear Sings help the seventeen-year-old Black Elk dramatize that part of the vision he called the horse dance. A sacred tepee is painted with pictures from his vision. There are four black horses and four white horses, four sorrels and four buckskins, a group for each of the four great directions, each horse with a young rider; and there are six very old men to represent the Six Grandfathers. Black Elk's vision recurs as the people act it out. Even the thunder beings attend the performance: rain and hail fall, and lightning flashes just a short distance from the dancers. The performance continues until everyone in the village has joined in the dancing; those without horses dancing on foot; everyone singing the vision songs together. At its conclusion, Black Road offers a prayer to the Powers of the world with the pipe and passes it around *until everyone in the whole village* has smoked at least one puff. Then Black Elk's fear is gone so that he is glad to see thunder clouds and the whole band feels happier and healthier, even those people who had been sick. Sharing of the vision through song and dance brings the people and Black Elk a sense of accomplishment and contentment. Even their horses respond with an increased sense of well-being (Neihardt, p. 179).

Then Black Elk goes through a long winter waiting for the thunder beings to reappear in the spring so he can do his next duty, which is to go out "lamenting" with the help of another old man, Few Tails. This lamenting, or praying for understanding, is so that "the spirits would hear me and make clear my next duty" (Neihardt, p. 186). As each duty is fulfilled, another duty arises. And yet the next duty is never clear; it must be clarified with the help of the elders. One must live out the vision to learn how to use the powers bestowed. This process of gradual maturity and awareness is carefully guided by the oldest and wisest men of one's nation and is supported by the whole community through its participation in the ritual enactments of the vision.

The holy man has to act in history and cannot avoid the agonizing attempt to understand what is being asked of him. How can he best use his powers on earth for the people? It is this aspect of Black Elk's visionary process which seems to me to be so instructive today. Black Elk's situation seems more difficult than most; to his credit, he neither becomes a fanatic, certain of the truth of his own understanding, nor does he give way to despair and hopelessness, but tries to understand how to put his vision to work in a world increasingly alien to it.

Black Elk is not one who knows, but *one who has been known* by the unknown in a terrifying and astonishing way. He always lives on the edge of what he calls "the beauty and the strangeness of the earth" (Neihardt, p. 277). He has been astonished, terrified, bewildered by that beauty and strangeness.

Black Elk receives another vision from his lamenting, the dog vision which he decides to perform with *heyokas,* sacred clowns, to make the people laugh, for "when people are already in despair, maybe the laughing face is better for them" (Neihardt, p. 193). A Holy Man named Poor takes charge of this ceremony for him with Black Elk himself performing as one of the clowns. The ceremony ends with the whole community rushing to a pot where the sacrificial dog has been boiled. Everyone tries to get a piece of the sacred flesh to eat. It is medicine to make them happier and stronger and:

> When the ceremony was over everybody felt a great deal better, for it had been a day of fun. They were better able now to see the greenness of the world, the wideness of the sacred day, the colors of the earth, and to set these in their minds. (Neihardt, p. 197)

Again, the effect of the ceremony is to reaffirm their sense of the unity of the world.

It is after the performance of the heyoka ceremony that Black Elk is first able to cure. He cures a small boy who has been very sick for a long time. Even so, he speaks of being afraid because he has never cured before, is unsure of his power, and, in fact, feels his way along as he works over the boy, pausing to think here and there until his doubts diminish and he understands better how to proceed. He tells us that he was so eager to cure this boy, that he called on "every power there is" although he knew that only one power would have been sufficient.

This summer of his first cure, another medicine man, Fox Belly, assisted him in performing his duty to that part of the vision that contained the power of the bison. After this ceremony, he felt more confident of himself, his doubt vanished, and he felt the power within him constantly and became busy curing the sick. The next summer he engaged the wise man, Running Elk, to help him perform the ceremony of the elk as his duty to that part of the vision. Whirlwind Chaser, Black Road, Bear Sings, Few Tails, Poor, Fox Belly, and Running Elk: these men are the elders, the carriers of the ancient wisdom, who guide and assist young Black Elk in the early stages of acting out his vision. They help him shape it into forms that bring it into the life of the community.

In the fall of 1883, the last of the great bison herds is slaughtered by the whites, and the Lakota are forced onto the reservation, wholly dependent on the government for issues of beef and flour. Black Elk continues curing for three years, but this power seems trivial in the face of his people's annihilation. "What are many little lives," he asks, "if the life of those lives be gone?" (Neihardt, p. 218) His despair is deep. He wishes to be able to heal the broken hoop of his nation and not simply the lives of individuals who are sick.

In the summer of 1886, recruiters for Buffalo Bill's Wild West show come to the Lakota looking for Indians to join their troupe and perform. Black Elk decides to go, motivated by the desire to see and understand the powerful world of the whites, in the hope that he will find some secret there to help him bring the sacred hoop back together again. This quest takes him to Omaha, Chicago, New York City, and across the ocean to England and France. Predictably, he finds nothing to help his people in any of these places because, as he says, the whites had forgotten that the earth was their mother and "had even the grass penned up":

> I looked back on the past and recalled my people's old ways, but they were not living that way any more. They were traveling the black road, everybody for himself and with little rules of his own, as in my vision. I was in despair, and I even thought that if the Wasichus had a better way, then maybe my people should live that way. (Neihardt, pp. 219–21)

Black Elk was gone for three years, during which he nearly died, and came back to the reservation to find things worse than ever before: drought, starvation, lies, the reservation reduced by a new treaty, the people pitiful and in despair. He was now without power, like a dead man, and could barely remember his vision. The news of the Ghost Dance reached his tribe that summer, and it was hard for him to believe. He listened all winter to accounts of the new religion, waited and wondered. His father died. He worked in a white man's store, puzzled, wondering if he should try to put the power of his vision and the power of this new religion together. The similarities seemed to be great. Finally he decided to go to a Ghost Dance. He saw the likenesses for himself, decided to enter into the new religion, and had new visions from which he made ghost shirts for many others.

He told his new vision through songs, the people weeping together for the beautiful world that had been taken from them. But eventually Black Elk came to feel misled by these new visions:

We danced there, and another vision came to me. I saw a Flaming Rainbow, like the one I had seen in my first great vision. Below the rainbow was a tepee of cloud. Over me there was a spotted eagle soaring, and he said to me: "Remember this." That was all I saw and heard.

I have thought much about this since, *and I have thought that this was where I made my great mistake.* I had had a very great vision, and I should have depended only upon that to guide me to the good. But I followed the lesser vision. . . . It is hard to follow one great vision in this world of darkness and of many changing shadows. Among those shadows men get lost [emphasis added]. (Neihardt, pp. 253–54)

Even holy men of vision make mistakes and temporarily lose their vision in the historical events of their time.

When Big Foot's band is slaughtered at Wounded Knee, Black Elk wants to die also. The heaps of bodies of women and children are too much for him. Later he wants to kill and get revenge. He is badly wounded in the stomach, but survives and even takes part in another skirmish two weeks later despite his wound.

Then begin the forty years of silence and desperation, which end when we hear his voice again through John Neihardt. It is no accident that Black Elk has nothing to say about the years between 1890 and 1930. Perhaps they were too painful for him to describe.[5]

The important elements, then, of this process of attempting to understand his vision, to do his duty to it, to release its power on earth in the life of his nation, are: (1) that it was not sought—it claimed him very early in his life; (2) that his initial response to it was fear and avoidance, the attempt to forget it; (3) that not to share it with the people of his tribe was to render it destructive, to turn its energy against him; (4) that sharing it involved him in an apprenticeship to the elders in his tribe and took up everyone in the immediate band as participants; (5) that having had a vision entailed grave duties and responsibilities to his people and to the world; and (6) that having a vision in no way guaranteed a sense of personal certainty, but demanded instead continuous attention to the *collective* process of unfolding its meaning and sharing that meaning with an ever-widening circle of people. This whole process, then, leads him to his final duty.

Black Elk's fundamental duty to his vision is always to seek understanding. As he says many times, "It is from understanding that power comes; and the power in the ceremony was in understanding what it meant" (Neihardt, p. 212). For him, the path to understanding is life long and difficult, beginning in fearfulness at the urgency with which the voices from his vision address him: "It is time! It is time!" Fearful because he does not know how to do what they want and fearful because although he had done his duty to the various parts of the vision, nevertheless, his nation had been devastated. But in the act of relinquishing his vision, *in giving it away,* he understands it on the deepest level.

As long as Black Elk held his vision close in the death-grip of his own cultural tradition, its power mocked him, just as it mocked him when he held it locked in his own private personality and made him think he was crazy. By letting it go its own way into the world, Black Elk acknowledges that the vision has a life of its own. And this life is not meant simply for him and his people, but for all peoples. Strangely this independent existence of the vision has been clearly expressed as a part of the original vision itself:

> I was seeing in a sacred manner the shapes of all things in the spirit, and shapes of all shapes as they must lie together like one being. And I saw that the sacred hoop of my peo-

ple was one of many hoops that made one circle, wide as daylight and as starlight, and in the center grew one mighty flowering tree to shelter all the children of one mother and one father. And I saw that it was holy. (Neihardt, p. 43)

The failure of the vision to protect and renew the life of his nation serves to show Black Elk that his understanding of the vision must move beyond the limits of his own culture. It is a painful realization, but it is this honesty in the face of limits that is so compelling about Black Elk. He never doubted that what he had experienced was real and powerful and true. He never felt that his vision and the sacred powers of the world were empty because they did not save his nation from a terrible history. Nor did he escape from the painful destruction of that history into his vision, calling it the only abiding reality and regarding the world and what happens in it insignificant by comparison. He startles us by his capacity to maintain the necessary interconnectedness between the physical, historical world, and the world of sacred powers of his vision. And Black Elk maintained this inter-connectedness under the pressure of great historical terror and despair.

Nicholas Black Elk waited at his historical dead-end forty years. Wondering, slowly going blind, never relinquishing his grip on either the world or the vision until there was a way to let them go together. The vision itself was to be twisted some in its transmission, filtered through the consciousness of John Neihardt, printed in a foreign tongue in a book to be read by people who had forgotten that the earth and sky and the four great directions are sacred ancestors. But in giving away his vision, Black Elk completed the great circle and affirmed that we are indeed all relatives. Ironically, it is historical terror, dislocation, and despair — these vehicles — that carry him that great distance, for without them, he might have stayed within the circle of his own culture.

We are at the center of the wisdom of Black Elk when we

understand this relatedness of all things in the circle of life in the act of giving away. There are four examples of giving away within Black Elk's narrative. The first two deal with giving away within the tribe; the other two extend that act to some part of the natural world.

In Black Elk's account of a Sun Dance, the warrior who counted coup on the tree that would be the center-pole proved his courage through his capacity to give to those in need: " . . . a warrior, who had done some very brave deed that summer, struck the tree, counting coup upon it; and when he had done this, he had to give gifts to those who had the least of everything, *and the braver he was, the more he gave away*" [emphasis added] (Neihardt, p. 96). Giving away, always the power of the circle, using one's power in the way the power of the world works, to express relatedness.

In preparing for the bison hunt,

the head man of the advisors went around picking out the best hunters with the fastest horses, and to these, he said: "Good young warriors, my relatives, your work I know is good. What you do is good always; so today you shall feed the helpless. Perhaps there are some old and feeble people without sons, or some who have little children and no man. You shall help these, and whatever you kill shall be theirs." This was a great honor for young men. (Neihardt, p. 56)

Giving away was a means of affirming that all are relatives in the great hoop of the world. In another place Black Elk and his father kill two deer:

While we were butchering, and I was eating some liver, I felt sorry that we had killed these animals and thought that we ought to do something in return. So I said: "Father, should we not offer one of these to the wild things?" He looked hard at me for a while. Then he placed one of the deer with its head to the east, and, facing the west, he raised his hands and cried: "Hey-hey" four times and prayed like this: "Grandfather, the Great spirit, behold me! To all the wild things that eat flesh, this I have offered that my people may live and the children grow up with plenty." (Neihardt, pp. 64–65)

The life of the wild things and the life of one's children are taken together here; they are not understood as belonging to separate realities. One must know how to give away, to foster in oneself and in one's people understanding of the way the power of the world works, or run the risk of exhaustion — of one's self, of one's people, of the world: "and the braver he was, the more he gave away." Perhaps this is expressed most strongly in Black Elk's description of the Oglala attitude toward death. (He explains why, upon entering a tepee, they went around a circle rather than directly to a certain place):

I can tell you something of the reason, but not all. Think of this: Is not the south the source of life, and does not the flowering stick truly come from there? And does not man advance from there toward the setting sun of his life? Then does he not approach the colder north where the white hairs are? And does he not then arrive, if he lives, at the source of light and understanding, which is the east? Then does he not return to where he began, to his second childhood, there to give back his life to all life, and his flesh to the earth whence it came? (Neihardt, pp. 203–204)

Sharing, giving away, giving back: These express his understanding of the great circle of relatedness that is the power of the world.

The knowledge of the circle informs the act of giving away.

So when Black Elk gives his vision away, he gives it back to the Grandfathers and to the great men of his tribe. In the preface of his book, we read:

What is good in this book
is *given back*
to the six Grandfathers
and
to the great men of my people [emphasis added].
(Neihardt, p. v)

Black Elk pays his debt in gratitude to the natural world and to the wise men of his tribe through the act of giving the vision away, transmitting it in the only way left to him. The logic is simple, impeccable, and rooted in the deepest tradition of his own culture, in the wisdom of the circle:

> You have noticed that everything an Indian does is in a circle, and that is because the Power of the World always works in circles, and everything tries to be round. . . . The sky is round, and I have heard that the earth is round like a ball, and so are all the stars. The wind, in its greatest power, whirls. Birds make their nests in circles, for theirs is the same religion as ours. The sun comes forth and goes down again in a circle. The moon does the same, and both are round. Even the seasons form a great circle in their changing, and always come back again to where they were. The life of a man is a circle from childhood to childhood, and so it is in everything where power moves. Our tepees were round like the nests of birds, and these were always set in a circle, the nation's hoop, a nest of many nests, where the Great Spirit meant for us to hatch our children.
> (Neihardt, pp. 198–200)

Nicholas Black Elk gives his most profound affirmation of his own tradition precisely in the act which seems to break most radically with it—giving the sacred knowledge to the invading whites — he breaks out of his historical dead-end by completing a very large circle, by sharing in an ever-widening orbit. Through this culminating act of giving away-giving back, he reaches beyond his own culture and history, creates a new beginning, and places squarely in our laps the first *duty* of all those who have received a great vision: the duty to seek understanding, understanding of how this vision (of the relatedness of all beings, which is sacred), can be made real, on earth, for all the people to see.

We will begin to take up the task of massive social/political change when we realize that the ongoing destruction of Indian people(s) is a direct reflection of what we have done to ourselves, to the first, original person in ourselves.

NOTES

1. The Wounded Knee slaughter was much more than just another example of a well-supplied army unit killing a band of Indians composed primarily of women, children, and old men. It was an act of revenge by Custer's old outfit, the Seventh Cavalry, waiting fourteen years since the Little Big Horn to get even with the Lakota. The president of the United States presented twenty-six Medals of Honor to the men of the Seventh Cavalry for their "bravery" at Wounded Knee Creek.

2. Letter, October 1940, Father Joseph A. Zimmerman, quoted in the publication of the Holy Rosary Mission, Pine Ridge Reservation, 1940.

3. This idea from a conversation with Joseph Epes Brown.

4. It is always summer when he is in direct contact with his vision. Summer is the time of intense storms on the Great Plains, with thunder and lightning, sudden winds, and rain. In fact, Black Elk likens his vision, and visions in general, to the energy of storms with their calm, fertile aftermath:

"When a vision comes from the thunder beings of the west, it comes with terror like a thunder storm; but when the storm of vision has passed, the world is greener and happier; for wherever the truth of vision comes upon the world, it is like a rain. The world, you see is happier after the terror of the storm." (Neihardt, p. 192)

5. These are the years of his work as a Catholic Catechist among the Lakota and other tribes. They are treated thoroughly by Raymond J. DeMallie in the introduction to his fine, *The Sixth Grandfather, Black Elk's Teachings Given to John G. Neihardt,* University of Nebraska Press, 1984.

Black Sun—Pure Light

Simon Ortiz in his poem, "For Our Brothers: Blue Jay, Gold Finch, Flicker, Squirrel" (Ortiz, pp. 128–131), sets before us the full impact of Euro-American society on North America, its life and people. These four creatures are the shattered remains of themselves, after being struck by cars on Colorado Highway 17. Ortiz refers to the events of their deaths as occurring in an "unnecessary war," and the brotherhood with them of the title is deep, for,

> Gold Finch, goddammit,
> the same thing is happening to us.

What makes the deaths of these bird and animal brothers even more devastating is that "nobody knows it"; they are "forgotten" in their lives as well as their deaths, except by the ants who are feeding on the decaying body of Blue Jay. Ortiz asks them

> . . . to do a good job,
> return Blue Jay completely

back into the earth,
back into the life.

The ants know more than merely the presence of the dead. Their knowledge is the knowledge of cycles, of life processes, decay being a process of return of one life back into other lives, or "into the life," as Ortiz says. The ants in this poem have more knowledge than the human beings who manufacture and drive the big machines at high speeds, and who create "the poorly made, cracked asphalt road" beside and on which these dead brothers lie.

But even here in the midst of this "unnecessary war," with the rotting, swollen, shattered bodies of his dead brothers, perhaps especially here because here it is most necessary, Ortiz manages passages of lyric intensity and beauty. As he looks at the remains of Blue Jay, the thought of him in flight comes to Ortiz:

the summer sunlight catching
a blade of wing, flashing
the bluegreen blackness,
the sun actually black, turning
into the purest flash of light.

It is this memory of the power of Blue Jay to transform the sun itself into "actually black" with its wing feathers, and to flash the purest light from that black sun, that astonishes us, especially in comparison to the shiny steel, plastic, and chrome of the speeding machines, flashy in a lesser sense, though Blue Jay, too, has been "in a mighty big hurry."

Ortiz's reference to the "unnecessary war" of this highway carnage of birds and animals is heightened by the fact that Blue Jay (also "Blue Crow") is associated with warfare by the Pueblos. Other features of Blue Jay for the Pueblos are his association with the direction west, the appearance of his feathers in the hair of Zuni priests on ceremonial occasions, on the prayer sticks of Zuni war priests before going on a raid, and when a house or field is dedicated (Tyler, pp. 255–56). And,

> In the Tewa pueblo of Tesuque, feathers of an unspecified jay are scattered on the ground or under stones in a shrine on a hill to the south. Because these offerings are made as a part of a Game dance, it is thought that they may be for the increase of game. (Tyler, p. 357)

It is clear from this that Blue Jay is a brother and more—a significant presence in the ceremonial life of Pueblo peoples. But his fearless swooping into the tall grasses and warlike cries make him no match for the speeding steel machines. The ministrations of the ants are a fitting "return" for his body, something of his spirit having released into that purest light of black sun off the wing blade.

From the dead body of Gold Finch, Ortiz takes "four tiny feathers," hoping to be blessed by the bird. He notices the "fading blood stain on a wing tip," bringing sorrow. He tells of his admiration for the yellow color of this bird, "the color of corn pollen," as it "glittered" in the tree branches. After mentioning how its voice would allow him to find it in the shade of his grandfather's peach tree, he again notes its color Gold Finch. A pollen bird / with tips of black."[1]

Here the yellow light of corn, of the sun, of Gold Finch, glittering among the leaves of the trees, with the light of his song "reasonably pretty and revealing" is like the flash of purest light from Blue Jay in its power to reveal the connections between things—peaches, corn, feathers, sun, moving yellow on the air like pollen, like warm light. And like Blue Jay, "forgotten, too, / the hard knots of gravel around / and under you."

With Flicker, the "proud brother" of the shortest section of this poem, Ortiz jams the language together in harsh repetition of the damage to bird bodies from hurtling steel machines:

Askew.
Head crushed.
Misshapen.
Mere chips of rotting wood
for your dead eyes.
Crushed.
Askew.
You always were one to fly
too close to flat, open ground.
Crushed.

By saying less about Flicker, and piling up the words "Crushed," "Askew," "Misshapen," he says more, actually intensifying the impact. And in the lines, "Your ochre wings were meant / for the prayer sticks," he gives the ritualistic importance of this bird, too. At A'coma, prayer sticks are regarded as gifts to the K'atsina.

"All important occasions must be preceded by, or accompanied with, the making and depositing of prayer sticks" might well be taken as a valid generalization of ceremonial procedure. They are made before all masked dances, the solstice ceremonies, at birth, and at death, for all ceremonial occasions are intimately concerned with the supernatural world, and prayer sticks are the most formal and satisfactory means of establishing the desired rapport with the spirits. (White, p. 69)[2]

Flicker, the "proud brother" was meant to have his rightful place in this ceremonial order of the Pueblo world, his ochre wings meant for the prayer sticks. The acknowledgment of that place makes his crushed body even more painful, for it expresses the damage to the order of Pueblo reality by the speeding machines and the society that puts its belief in them, in its capacity to make them from the "raw material" of the earth.

Squirrel is last. Again, there is the detailed knowledge of the animal's life, its sudden and gray "flashing" as it runs, its "shrieks of sound." Again, there is the soft vegetable world, this time "underbrush oak" rather than cottonwood or peach trees, or "the tall dry grasses" of Blue Jay. "One dim eye" stares across the road at these oaks it can neither see nor reach. As Ortiz tries to lift its body into the high grass it comes apart. "It is glued heavily / to the ground with its rot" so that he has to push it into the grass with his foot,

> . . . being careful
> that it remains upright
> and is facing the rainwater
> that will wash it downstream.

This care in the handling of the rotting remains of the quashed squirrel, keeping it upright and facing the rainwater, expresses his reverence for its life, even at this unsavory extreme. His response to its remains is ritualistic in the simplest, most direct meaning of that term. He extends this into the next lines where he smells its rot "and wipe[s] its fur on my fingers / off with a stone / with a prayer for it / and murmur[s] a curse." He does not recoil from the smell nor the touch of its decaying flesh. It must be accorded the respect due to the remains of any living thing. That is without question. Those who have forgotten this in their speeding machines along the poorly made, cracked asphalt, have disturbed this ceremonially ordered world, and appear ignorant of or aloof from any awareness of their impact. His anger, sorrow, and puzzlement are clear. But the poem ends powerfully, affirming the importance of doing "this much" for them, and more —

knowing your names, telling about you.

He cannot change their deaths, and the conditions that caused them, but he is far from helpless in the face of them. For his knowledge of their names, and lives, and his ability to tell their story, as well as his care for their remains, allows him to express the meaning of and respect for their lives, and to present a way of living that does not *necessitate* the ignorant sacrifice of innocent forms of life in the pursuit of our ends. Perhaps it is the ignorance, and the forgetting, of this destruction that is the real terror of it: the total lack of regard for those we have crushed along our way. In this poem Ortiz gives meaning to the term "brothers" as applied to birds and animals through the pain, sorrow, and anger he feels at their deaths, and the care with which he knows their lives and handles their remains.

It is clear from our examination of the underlying ritualistic element in Ortiz's poem that he has been able to keep his poetry open to its roots in ancient Pueblo culture. What is even more striking about Ortiz's work is that the animals of the poem are obviously literally real, and to take them only in their mythic, symbolic, or metaphoric meanings, as a sort of poetic way of understanding them, is to reduce the reality of their living and dying to the conceptual categories of Euro-American literary consciousness.

NOTES

1. The significance of pollen, especially corn pollen, in the Pueblos is widely known. Parsons, in her report of work at Isleta, states,

Corn meal or pollen (our informant uses the terms indiscriminately) is in very general ritual use. It is sprinkled by everybody to the sun at sunrise. In ceremonial it is sprinkled to sun, moon, stars. It is sprinkled in all directions, or in the direction of any spirit that is being addressed. It is sprinkled on prayer feathers, on the altar, and on the sun spot. It is placed in the basket or on the hand where sacrosanct objects are to be placed or given. It is thrown in the river or buried in the field. The meal and pollen are contained separately in buckskin in the pouch of the bandoleer. Corn pollen only is used; not as in some other places pollen from flowers. Corn pollen may be gathered by anybody, "with a song," asking one of the cornstalks in the row for it. "We always ask for what we gather."

Parsons, Elsie Clews. *Isleta, New Mexico.* Annual Reports of Bureau American Ethnology, Vol 47, pp. 275–76.

2. And at the summer solstice ceremony,

everyone makes prayer sticks to be deposited on the morning of the solstice. Each person makes four sticks which are tied together and wrapped in a corn husk. On the morning of the solstice, two men and two women take the sticks for all the people to the east side of the cliff and offer them to the sun and to the K'obictaiya.

And during the winter solstice ceremony, on

the third day before the solstice, the men take their prayer sticks out to their fields and bury them; the women carry theirs to the east edge of the mesa and throw them down. (White, p. 85)

And at a death ceremony

the father makes four prayer sticks, painted black, which he puts in the right hand of the deceased. Then he makes four more which he puts in a pottery bowl, together with four made by the mother. . . . Four days after the death, a medicine man, solicited with corn meal by the father of the deceased, takes a burnt stick which has been placed where the deceased lay, the prayer sticks made by the father and the mother, and a "lunch," and goes to the grave, where he prays. Then he goes down the sand trail to the foot of the mesa, and then to the north. He goes out to some mesa or canyon, where he deposits his burden. The sticks are for Iatik [the All-Mother]. (White, pp. 137–38)

APPENDIX

For Our Brothers:
Blue Jay, Gold Finch, Flicker, Squirrel
by Simon Ortiz
Acoma Pueblo

Who perished lately in this most unnecessary war, saw them lying off the side of a state road in southwest Colorado

They all loved life.
And suddenly,
it just stopped for them. Abruptly,
the sudden sound of a speeding
machine,
and that was it.

Blue Jay. Lying there,
his dry eyelids are tiny scabs.
Wartstones, looking ugly.
His legs are just old sticks,
used to push ashes away.

O goddammit, I thought,
just lying there.
Thought of the way he looks,
swooping in a mighty big hurry,
gliding off a fence pole
into a field of tall dry grass,
the summer sunlight catching
a blade of wing, flashing
the bluegreen blackness,
the sun actually black, turning
into the purest flash of light.
And so ugly now, dead.
And nobody knows it except
for those black ants crawling
into and out of decaying entrails.
Nobody but those ants,
and I ask them to do a good job,
return Blue Jay completely
back into the earth,
back into the life.

Gold Finch, I took four tiny feathers
from your broken body.
I hope you were looking at me then
out of that life, perhaps
from the nearest hills
from that young cottonwood tree.
I hope you blessed me.
Until I looked very closely,
I didn't see the fading blood stain
on a wing tip, and I sorrowed for you.
I have always been one to admire
the yellow, the color of corn pollen,
on your tiny feathers as I've seen

you glittering from branch to branch,
whirring and rushing from one tree
to another. I have seen the yellow
of your tiny body and the way
the shades of the cottonwood
and my grandfather's peach trees
could hide you so well
but in a moment your voice
would always speak
and you could be found.
Gold Finch. A pollen bird
with tips of black, flits
his head around and sings
reasonably pretty and revealing.
There you were, forgotten too,
the hard knots of gravel around
and under you, lying besides
the poorly made, cracked asphalt
road upon which sped that hunk
of steel, plastic and chrome.
Well, I'm sorry for the mess.
I'll try to do what I can
to prevent this sort of thing
because, Gold Finch, goddammit,
the same thing is happening to us.

Flicker, my proud brother.
Your ochre wings were meant
for the prayer sticks.
Askew.
Head crushed.
Misshapen.
Mere chips of rotting wood
for your dead eyes.
Crushed.

Askew.
You always were one to fly
too close to flat, open ground.
Crushed.

Squirrel, a gray thing
with bits of brown
where tiny ears join its head.
Eats seeds, nuts, tender roots,
tiny savory items.
Runs quickly, flashing gray
and sudden.
Throws its head with jerky
nervous motion.
Flicks hardwood shrieks of sound.
Lying by the side of Highway 17,
staring with one dim eye across
the road at underbrush oak,
its body swollen with several days
of death in the hot sun,
its tail a distorted limp twist.
I touch it gently and then try to lift it, to toss it
into some high grass,
but its fur comes loose.
It is glued heavily
to the ground with its rot
and I put my foot
against it and push it
into the grass, being careful
that it remains upright
and is facing the rainwater
that will wash it downstream.
I smell the waste
of its disintegration
and wipe its fur on my fingers

off with a stone
with a prayer for it
and murmur a curse.

I don't have to ask who killed you.
I know and I am angry and sorry
and wonder what I shall do.

This, for now, is as much as I can do,
knowing your names, telling about you.
Squirrel. Flicker. Gold Finch. Blue Jay.
Our brothers.

Fusion

"The soul is composed of the external world."
— Wallace Stevens

The local, external world (the land and all the life-forms that rise up from it) is internalized as a matter of survival necessity by native peoples. And it is this internalization that gives to native peoples their power and beauty, the rightness of their existence. We call this inner/outer fusion, "harmony with the natural world." But the terms "internal" and "external" are themselves already the product of the separated consciousness that characterizes Western civilization — and civilization in general. It is as accurate to say that native peoples are called out of themselves by the beauty and diversity of the natural world as it is to say that they internalize it.

Rather than internalization or externalization, let us say that native peoples, Kalahari Bushmen, say, are the desert as it articulates itself through human form and culture. And the desert is the Bushman as he articulates himself through natural form. They *are* together. They are one. They partake of the same is, or being. They do not make sense in separation from each other. The desert without its Bushman, every bit as much as the Bushman without his desert, is emptied, reduced in its capacity to express itself, to be itself. This is not to say that the other desert life-forms are insignificant — they too are the desert, are the Bushmen. But there is a human way of the desert that fulfills the desert, every bit as much as there is a desert way of the human that fulfills the human being.

All that one really need know in order to understand the lives and cultures of native peoples lies in the meaning of the small word "of." If one understands at a deep level what it means to be of the desert, or of the Arctic, or of the bison or deer or salmon or reeds, one understands native peoples and this fusion between them and local place. The first one hundred pages or so of Laurens van der Post's *The Heart of the Hunter* contains a powerful account of native people being "of" the desert. The remainder of this essay will be an explication of the superb second chapter of his book.

At the end of Chapter One, and throughout Chapter Two, van der Post, with the help of an invincible steenbuck, a Bushman woman and child, an old Bushman grandfather, and the Kalahari Desert, takes us inside the deep interpenetration between Bushman and desert that is the underlying power of their existence. Van der Post is on his way out of the Kalahari after spending some days with a small band of Bushmen at a place named the "sip wells." He runs across another band of eighteen people. An old couple has just that day been left behind, too weakened with thirst and hunger to go on. A woman goes back with water for them, and an hour and a half later they walk into camp. It is a day in which van der Post experiences "the magic of the steenbuck," emptying the magazine of his rifle at a fine specimen not twenty yards away without hitting it, and spends the first night in his life actually camped among a group of "wild" Bushmen in the desert. At night, away from the campfire, he stumbles onto a lone woman holding her child "high above her head, and singing something, with her own face lifted to the sky" (van der Post,

p. 32). He's told by Dabé, his Bushman interpreter, that "she's asking the stars to take the little heart of her child and to give him something of the heart of a star in return," because "the stars up there have heart in plenty and are great hunters. She is asking them to take from her little child his little heart and to give him the heart of a hunter" (van der Post, p. 33). The woman greets him and Dabé and takes them to her fire; he makes the rounds of other fires as well until he comes to the old couple who had been left behind that day, having some "man's talk" with their grandchildren. And van der Post, too, stays for some man's talk, the only moment in his book when an old Bushman speaks his own world directly to us (albeit through van der Post and Dabé). Van der Post, true Western European that he is, has questions: "Was it true that the stars were hunters?" "Did the little steenbuck really possess great magic, and if so, what sort of magic?" (van der Post, p. 38). His questions are met with a long silence. (This silence appears in all true accounts of questioning exchange between those from European backgrounds and those from native backgrounds and is inseparable from the contents of any answers that are forthcoming. It is like the silence of the night which contains the language of the stars.) Van der Post speaks of previous conversations with Bushmen, and of some of the old stories they've shared with him. The old man finally begins to speak. Yes, it is true, the stars are all hunters, but some are greater than others. The old man points to the brightest star in the Great Dipper and says it is:

> a great hunter who hunted in far away dangerous places in the shape of a lion. Could I not see how fierce its eye shone and hear the distant murmur of its roar? . . . The greatest hunter was not there yet. It hunted in the darkest and most dangerous places of all, so far away that we could not see it yet. We could see it only in the early morning when it came nearer on its way home. There, there was a hunter for you!

The old father made a lively whistling sound of wonder at the greatness of the hunter. Yes, just before dawn one could see him striding over the horizon, his eye bold and shining, an arrow ready in his bow. When he appeared, the night whisked around to make way for him, the red dust spurting at its black heels. He broke off and shook his grey old head, as he once more uttered that sound of wonder, before asking as if the thought had just come to him: "But can't you hear for yourself the cries of the hunt going on up there?" (van der Post, pp. 39–40)

The first time I read this passage, I was moved by its beauty, but my skepticism was also aroused: I had not heard the stars. I suppose I considered it poetically quaint that the Bushmen should "project" their hunting concerns onto the stars. It was just such accounts as this, I thought, that had led to the rejection or romantization of native peoples and their experience. Native peoples appear to be natively animistic, or to anthropomorphize nature without knowing it. Stars neither speak nor hunt, I thought. They will never truly understand the stars until they disengage from this projecting of their own concerns onto them. But my skepticism, too, was not satisfying, for it expressed a kind of closure on a world that was real, was there in the experience of native peoples, and I wanted to understand that world. As I taught the book, more than one student spoke of experiencing the stars speaking while sleeping out in natural places. I began to ponder about meaning, about how things come to mean what they do, about the shape meaning has for us. At some point, my skepticism began to dissolve, or at least to become unimportant in comparison to the world-experience I was trying to understand. The skepticism was not wrong, but it was blocking. As a man from Euro-American civilization, not as a Bushman, I came to understand in the following manner.

Meaning must occur in terms that make sense to us, in terms that have to do with our actual life — conditions. Meaning does not occur either in some sort of experiential vacuum, or in terms that are divorced from our actual concerns and condition. To the extent that this is so, we must be cautious about labelling as "projections" those experiences of other peoples that are expressed in terms suitable to their circumstances — that the stars are great hunters is an appropriate response from a hunting-gathering culture in a desert where sky is as vast and powerful as any ocean. (Skepticism itself may be suitable to the circumstances of Euro-American civilization in the twentieth century, but there is little historical or cultural solace in that!)[1]

If survival for native peoples necessitated, as I believe it does, the dissolving of the borders betwen inner and outer worlds, necessitated becoming radically "of" the desert or the deer, then the means of establishing this linkage, the means of becoming "of" particular places and species, of creating a fusion between inner and outer worlds such that every Bushman carries the whole Kalahari Desert in its minute particulars within him, is story telling. The story that takes up with the place or other life-form in ways that relate the humans to the place or life-form, that expresses the human being's condition, concerns, circumstances, is the most precious cultural creation there is. And such story telling is neither mere personification, nor subjectivity, nor projection. It is based on sheer survival necessity through creating meaning out of one's relationship to the world. Without this creation of meaningful story as the literal fabric or flesh of one's interrelationship with the world one is set adrift and either does not survive, or survives in despair, depression, anxiety, wantonness or, I'm tempted to say, skepticism, which has its own story. What it means to be of the desert is to have so opened one's being or spirit to all the particulars of that place that the events of the desert take place within oneself every bit as much as out there in the natural world. Van der Post states it exactly:

> When one has lived as close to nature for as long as we had done, one is not tempted to commit the metropolitan error of assuming that the sun rises and sets, the day burns out and the night falls, in a world outside oneself. These are great and reciprocal events, which occur also in ourselves. (van der Post, p. 93)

And so, the story about the stars as hunters.

At the end of a Kalahari Bushman film entitled *The Hunters,* the returning men, after a thirteen-day hunt, tell the story of the hunt. And part of the story is the distribution of the meat they have brought, how it is shared out among the band. The story itself is like the meat, is the meat. The hunt itself is not complete until everyone has been nourished by the story of the hunt, until the whole tale has been handed out to children and women and old people and all those others who did not go. What is brought back is far more than the literal meat of a giraffe, necessary as that is. What is brought back and distributed to the people with the meat is the experience itself, shaped in story by the hunters. The distribution of the meat is the literal, physical expression of the distribution of *the whole journey itself.* The capacity of storytelling is somehow integral to the capacity for the journey, or hunt, in native cultures where there is a much greater collective sense than among us. Not everyone who ventures out onto the veld will be a storyteller, but someone among those hunters must be if the journey itself is to nurture the whole band and not just those few who go. The hunt, after all, is not for food for just the four who go. It is for food for their wives that their breasts may fill with milk for their children. It is for food for their parents who are now too old to hunt. (The first arrow to hit the giraffe was made by an old man, too old to hunt, so when the hunters returned, they honored him with a large amount of meat, that he might have the pleasure of distributing it to all those not directly related to the hunters.) The power of storytelling is two-fold then. It carries the meaningful linkage to the world and experience, and it is the means of sharing that world and experience with those too young or old or incapacitated to go.

When human beings are "of" their local world, centered in and by it, their stories are filled with experiences of star hunters, deer people, rain people, insect allies. They have found, there in their particular place in the world, those with whom to compose and nourish their souls. They have established or participated in the great, on-going dialogue or conversation of everything with everything in their place. We do not hear the stars. In the words of Martin Heidegger, things don't "thing" for us. The noise of our own society and central nervous system fills the airwaves — all else is jammed. We talk incessantly because we have forgotten how much there is to hear. (A student once told my class that her grandfather always said the reason we have two ears but only one tongue is because we're supposed to listen at least twice as much as we talk.)

If one pursues the imagery of the stars as hunters of the Bushman grandfather, one discovers that a large part of the power of the stars, for the Bushmen, is their capacity to endure darkness and distance. Those who hunt in the darkest parts of the sky, and so far off it is nearly dawn when they return, are the bravest hunters. The sun has the power to vanquish darkness, but the stars must accept it as their medium; they are mere splinters of light flung out into the vast darkness of deep space. The Bushmen attribute to them great courage for their ability to maintain the pure intensity of their light in the midst of this dark ocean. To ask that the heart of one's own child be exchanged with the heart of a star means not only will the child be a great hunter, possessed of the courage to endure darkness and distance, but its own heart will reside among the stars, establishing the supportive relationship with the universe that will see him through many a far, dark night. What a gift to have as an example of how to be — to live with a star's heart in oneself, to know one's own heart shines in the night sky, to be the child of such an exchange. "The soul is composed of the external world." What comparable examples of sustaining linkage to the natural world does modern civilization offer to its children?

Personification. Projection. Animism. Myth. These are precisely the vehicles for establishing meaningful linkage between human beings and the universe. But we have not addressed the actual cries of the hunt going on up in the night sky. Do the stars actually speak? Van der Post's interpreter Dabé, fearing that van der Post looks on his experience of the stars speaking as childish, blurts, "Surely you must know that the stars are great hunters? Can't you hear them? Do listen to what they are crying! Come on! Moren! You are not so deaf you cannot hear them." Van der Post responds,

> I have slept out under the stars in Africa for too many years not to know that they sound and re-sound in the sky. From the time I was born until I first went to school, I slept outside a house every night except when it was raining — and that was seldom. My first memories are of the incomparable starlight of the high veld of Southern Africa and the far sea-sound that goes with it.

> I hastened to say, "Yes, Dabé, of course I hear them!" But then I was forced to add, "Only I do not know what they are saying. Do you know?"

> Reassured, he stood for a moment, head on one side, while the light of another flash from the horizon flew like a ghost moth by us. Then, with the note of indulgence he could not resist using on me when he felt his authority not in doubt,

he said, "They are very busy hunting tonight and all I hear are their hunting cries: 'Tssik!' and 'Tsa!'"

Had it not been for the darkness between us, he would have seen, I am sure, the shock of amazement on my face. I had known those sounds all my life. Ever since I can remember, we ourselves had used them out hunting with our dogs. "Tssik!" repeated sharply thrice was the sound we used to alert our dogs when we were at the cover of bush, grass, cave, or donga in which we suspected our quarry to be hiding. Hearing it, the ears of our dogs would immediately prick up, their eyes shine with excitement, and their noses sniff the air diligently for scent. Another "Tssik" would send them to search the cover. "Tsa" was the final imperative note which released them from all restraint and launched them after our chosen quarry when it was flushed.

I had always wondered about the origin of these sounds. Neither of them had ever seemed European to me. I had asked the oldest of the old people of all races and colours. I asked one of the greatest of all African hunters, too. They could only say that, like me, they had been born into a world in which they were already in long-established use. Stranger still, wherever I went in the world, I found that, although hunters outside Africa did not know the sounds and therefore, did not use them with their dogs, if I tried them out, many of the dogs responded. They would start searching with all their senses: if I kept up the sounds for long, they became exceedingly restless, in the end letting out that involuntary and nostalgic whimper normally provoked in them only by the moon. That had deepened the mystery for me, but now I thought I knew: we had the sounds from the Bushman, and he and the dogs had them straight from the stars. (van der Post, pp. 33–34)

What is interesting about this passage is that van der Post has no doubt about the experience of sound in the night sky in Africa, nor about the stars being the source of that sound. His problem is that he does not know how to translate this star sound into meaning for himself, and so it is merely sound resounding in the sky. But the Bushmen have translated that sound into meaningful words, into hunting cries: Tssik! and Tsa! and though van der Post has heard these as hunters' commands to dogs his whole life and is shocked at that recognition, he never does say that he can hear these specific commands, Tssik! and Tsa! from the stars. But he does realize that hunters and their dogs all over Africa have a mutually intelligible set of commands which the Bushmen experience as having come from the stars. What is important here is that a meeting has occurred between Bushmen and stars, that sound is the event through which they meet, and out of this meeting through sound, human language has arisen. What is important is the experience that language comes to us every bit as much as it comes from us. It makes our own Biblical statement that "in the beginning was the word" ring with a sense of origins beyond mere human creativity. If one couples this experience of language as coming to us from the stars (and other life forms) with the fact that Bushman speech, like that of most native languages, is markedly onomatopoeic, then it becomes clear that one source of language lies in the human reception of and response to the sounds of the world and that the truest languages may be those that never depart far from sounding like what has been heard.

A primary source of renewal, then, for a language is through silence, the silence of the human voice and machinery so that the sounds of other life forms may return to our ears. Our language becomes impoverished to the extent it closes itself off from the natural world and from silence, and insists that it is a purely human phenomenon. It becomes increasingly technical as this is done. If the stars did not speak, then neither would we. Our speech is in response to an older, more primordial speaking.

Van der Post's questioning of the Bushman grandfather about the magic of the steenbuck is even more revealing. The old man's immediate response is to sit up "and beat the sand with the side of his hand for emphasis." Of course the steenbuck had magic, great magic! Surely everyone knew that; even the children, like his grandsons there, knew it.

"But, old father, I insisted, I do not know it. What sort of magic is it? What does it do?" (van der Post, p. 42) Van der Post paraphrases the "old father's" response.

I gathered that the magic of the steenbuck was that of the innocent, the gentle, and the beautiful combined in one. It was a creature — or a person[2] as he called it — too beautiful to be aware of imperfection, too innocent to know fear, too gentle to suspect violence. How it differed from the duiker! Had I not noticed that the heart of the duiker was full of suspicion and fear? At the first strange sound, it assumed the worst and bounded away as fast as it could without a backward glance. The steenbuck, however, when disturbed would stand up and slip out quietly from its "place which it made more prettily than any other animal on the veld and wherein it always feels itself to be lying so nicely." It would stand quietly beside "its place" and look without fear out of its great eyes, its "little ears trembling and nicely pointed" to see what the wonderful noise could be about. The old father's eyes as he spoke seemed to become young and eager like the steenbuck's, his own Pan-like ear to point and tremble with innocent curiosity. The steenbuck, he said, would stand there all the time "looking so nicely and acting so prettily" that the person who had come hunting it would begin to feel "he must look nicely at the steenbuck and act prettily too." The person who had come to hunt it would suddenly find there was "a steenbuck person" behind him who "feeling that he was looking nicely at the little buck, wanted him to act nicely and prettily too." When the person who had come to kill the steenbuck fitted the arrow to his bow and aimed to shoot, the steenbuck person behind him "pulled at his arm and made him miss." Yes, that was the magic of the steenbuck; it had a steenbuck person to protect it.

I should perhaps have left the matter there, but I could not resist an obvious question. Why if that were so, I asked, was the steenbuck ever killed? He looked at me almost in pity. . . . Yes, he agreed in the end, steenbuck were killed in spite of their magic, just as the duiker was killed in spite of its speed and suspiciousness. Yet more steenbuck survived than were killed. Certainly in all his long years, its numbers had never become less. How could so small and defenseless an animal have survived in a world full of powerful enemies without great magic? His old eyes were suddenly childlike with mischief and he looked past me, as if he saw "a steenbuck person" standing beside me, to say he had been told I had tried hard that very morning to kill a little steenbuck and failed. Perhaps he had been misinformed, but if not. . . . (van der Post, pp. 41–42)

Who is this steenbuck person standing behind the hunter, making him miss? It appears to us that he is a part of the hunter himself, the hunter's own capacity for the innocent, the gentle, and the beautiful combined in one and aroused in response to the animal. The presence of the steenbuck awakens these in the hunter. The presence of the steenbuck creates a reciprocal presence within the hunter—the hunter's own "steenbuckness." If the hunter has managed to destroy or repress these qualities within himself (as many modern hunters seem able to do), he will be able to destroy them when he meets them in the person of the steenbuck. The sadness of this description lies in the extent to which modern hunting appears to have precluded, for many, this establishment of a reciprocal relatedness to the hunted animal that has the power to change or affect the hunter. Long-range weaponry gives us the power to kill from outside the reach of the animal's being. But if these qualities of innocence, beauty, and gentleness are still alive in the hunter, the actual steenbuck is perfectly formed to connect with them — to spoil his aim. Missing the steenbuck is a way, unconsciously we would say, of keeping alive these qualities within himself, of affirming them. "The soul is composed of the external world." (Stevens)

But if the steenbuck person is merely an external form of some inner qualities of the hunter, why is it that the Bushmen speak of experiencing him as outside, as at their elbow? When we, with our modern psychological understanding, move the steenbuck person from behind the hunter (at his elbow) to within him, we thereby reduce the reality-presence of the steenbuck and of the natural world. We subsume their reality under the category of the human subconscious. No mystification is intended here, but in the interest of speaking for the reality-presence of other life-forms, of the steenbuck, as having powerful existences of their own, it seems wise to leave the steenbuck person outside the hunter, at his elbow, lest he be swallowed up by the gargantuan self-importance of modern man. Outside, he remains as a presence we encounter and engage from a radically other life, the life of the desert steenbuck. He is primordially a part of that, and linked to us by his touch, which spoils our aim. Inside us, he would begin to disappear. The Bushmen in their wisdom situate him in the desert from which he came and where he belongs. By virtue of this, they acknowledge a new reality created out of the meeting between Bushmen and steenbuck, just as language was created out of the meeting between Bushmen and stars. All this comes from an experience of reality as occurring neither in the external world of nature nor in the subjective creations of man, but in the meeting of the two.

Furthermore, those qualities of the innocent, the gentle, and the beautiful are read from keen, detailed observation which is at pains to learn the characteristics of specific species and to distinguish them from other species, as the steenbuck is distinguished from the duiker because of behavioral differences. The hunter has kept open to taking in the particulars of this kind of buck right here in front of him now, and to the particulars of individual animals — taking them in and allowing them to resound inside himself. The fact that we can machine gun steenbuck (and Bushmen) from air-conditioned Land Rovers attests merely to our callousness, separation, closure, to our having first destroyed within ourselves the innocent, the gentle, and beautiful.

A society of those who have effectively silenced their capacity to respond to the stars or the steenbuck, of those who have so separated themselves from the rest of nature as to think and feel and actually believe that they alone have full consciousness or spirit or value in and of themselves, is the most dangerous and potentially destructive society imaginable.

The fundamental truth of our existence that the old Bushman father and the Kalahari Desert offer us is that our lives are thoroughly reciprocal; there is a steenbuck person at our elbow, touching us from within the heart of beauty, gentleness, and innocence, even as we take aim with our weapons at this very one.

NOTES

1. cf. Appendix I for a Bushman story that captures precisely the place we are now historically.
2. Note on the use of the term "person" in reference to deer, trees, insects, rain, etc. The objection sometimes raised to

this term states that deer are simply deer, not people. To use the term "person" in reference to them is to project or impose human or human-like qualities onto them rather than to see them as they are, in their own various existences. Better to leave the "person" term entirely out of it than to open up our view of other life-forms to this human-centric reference.

To be sure, it is essential not to impose or project human-like qualities onto the other life-forms, even by implication and with the good intention of recognizing their primary right to exist as and for themselves. However, while it is important to respect the integrity of other life-forms as distinct from human life, the differences between our existence and theirs have been understood so as to allow us to forget the other half of this truth; i.e., that there are primary ways in which we share existence with them. By insisting on the difference between our existence and theirs, we have denied them the qualities of intelligence, feeling, and soul, and have consequently reduced them to mere material to be handled by us for our own ends in whatever ways we are able. We must be painstaking in our efforts not to impose upon them even as we attempt to re-establish our ancient linkage to them.

At this point, it might be asked, how is it that the life of a steenbuck or insect or rock is equal to or as important as my life? After all, I have more intelligence, more choices; I am more powerful, can kill or use them if I wish. I write articles, teach in a university, etc. How can the existence of a "lower" life-form be as important as mine? The Bushman grandfather, in his view of the steenbuck as a person, is either a fool engaging in naive projection, or he is tricking us, or van der Post has misunderstood, or mis-translated his words.

In order to answer this question, we must look to the oral traditions of native peoples worldwide. What we discover in these traditions is story after story bearing witness to the power or spirit residing in all other life-forms, from insects and rocks to rain and stars. These various powers or spirits come to human beings at special times in their lives: in dreams, in moments of great crisis, sickness, or pain, at puberty, during vision quests, or simply when the person is alone and at one with the natural world. The testimony of persons from oral-tradition societies everywhere, always, is that they directly experience individuals from other life-forms as persons who come to them and from whom they receive gifts of knowledge and power. Their societies and their personal lives are centered, guided, and sustained by this experience of deep communication with other life-forms. It would not occur to members of a subsistence society that they were extending the concept of person to a non-human life-form. This would be far too human-centered for them. Their recognition of members of other life-forms as persons is a natural, logical part of their experience of and communication with them. Intelligence, emotion, soul — these are not experienced as being the exclusive properties of human beings, but as residing in all the life-forms with which we share the world, and those human beings to whom the person of rain or ant or snake or star has not presented itself are left vulnerable as a result.

The real question here is, what is it that makes us so sure that the ancient human experience of the other life-forms as persons is merely a projection of human characteristics onto them? Does not the very pain and numbness of our alienation express our recognition that our "certainty" here is inaccurate, is not capable of supplying us with the basic necessities of existence, is, indeed, a violation of the needs of our own spirit for primal connection to the world? After all, who are these other life-forms if not the ancient nations of the earth, those very ones whose bodies we journeyed through on our long, evolutionary path to ourselves? Do we not carry within ourselves all those ancient life-forms we've lived through in becoming human? Dare we deny these ancient ancestors their rightful place in existence? The sheer ingratitude to these old grandfathers and grandmothers is so immense as to blind us. We do not realize there is anyone to be grateful to.

The "arrogance of humanism" is based on a short-term memory. If the oral tradition does one thing, it is to exercise the power of memory to an astonishing extent — it remembers the human ancestry far back in evolutionary time. When the Bushman mother holds her child up to the starry African night and asks that it be given the heart of a star, she is acknowledging that her child and the stars are one — made of the same star material. After all, the sun, our close star, is the source of all life on this earth.

Native peoples, peoples of oral tradition worldwide and as far back as human memory can reach, have acknowledged their respect for and communication with all the other life-forms through this most simple and direct form of expression — the concept of the person. We understand instinctively that to be a person is to have rights, independence of existence, equality, and significance. When the critics of this ancient term of respect for other life-forms come up with a better way of simple, direct acknowledgment of all that is implied by it, then it will be time to change or drop the term.

APPENDIX

From *The Heart of the Hunter* by Laurens van der Post.

The man of the early race . . . she told me, dearly loved his black and white cattle. He always took them out into the veld himself, chose the best possible grazing for them, and watched over them like a mother over her children, seeing that no wild animals came near to hurt or disturb them. In the evening, he would bring them back to his kraal, seal the entrance carefully with branches of the toughest thorn, and watching them contentedly chewing the cud, think, "In the morning I shall have a wonderful lot of milk to draw from them." One morning, however, when he went into his kraal, expecting to find the udders of the cows full and sleek with milk, he was amazed to see they were slack, wrinkled, and empty. He thought with immediate self-reproach he had chosen their grazing badly, and took them to better grass. He brought them home in the evening and again thought, "Tomorrow for certainty I shall get more milk than ever before." But again in the morning the udders were slack and dry. For the second time, he changed their grazing, and yet again the cows had no milk. Disturbed and suspicious, he decided to keep a watch on the cattle throughout the dark.

In the middle of the night, he was astonished to see a cord of finely-woven fibre descending from the stars; and down this cord, hand over hand, one after another, came some young women of the people of the sky. He saw them, beautiful and gay, whispering and laughing softly among themselves, steal into the kraal and milk his cattle dry with calabashes. Indignant, he jumped out to catch them, but they scattered cleverly so that he did not know which way to run. In the end, he did manage to catch one; but while he was chasing her, the rest, calabashes and all, fled up the sky, withdrawing the cord after the last of them so that he could not follow. However, he was content because the young woman he had caught was the loveliest of them all. He made her his wife, and from that moment, he had no more trouble from the women of the people of the sky.

His new wife now went daily to work in the fields for him while he tended his cattle. They were happy, and they prospered. There was only one thing that worried him. When he caught his wife, she had a basket with her. It was skillfully woven, so tight that he could not see through it, and was always closed firmly on top with a lid that fitted exactly into the opening. Before she would marry him, his wife had made him promise that he would never lift the lid of the basket and look inside until she gave him permission to do so. If he did, a great disaster might overtake them both. But, as the months went by, the man began to forget his promise. He became steadily more curious, seeing the basket so near day after day, with the lid always firmly shut. One day when he was alone, he went into his wife's hut, saw the basket standing there in the shadows, and could bear it no longer. Snatching off the lid, he looked inside. For a moment he stood there unbelieving, then burst out laughing.

When his wife came back in the evening, she knew at once what had happened. She put her hand to her heart, and looking at him with tears in her eyes, she said, "You've looked in the basket."

He admitted it with a laugh, saying, "You silly woman. You silly, silly creature. Why have you made such a fuss about this basket? There's nothing in it at all."

"Nothing?" she said, hardly finding the strength to speak.

"Yes, nothing," he answered emphatically.

At that she turned her back on him, walked away straight into the sunset and vanished. She was never seen on earth again.

To this day, I can hear the old black servant woman saying to me, "And do you know why she went away, my little master? Not because he had broken his promise, but because looking into the basket he had found it empty. She went because the basket was not empty: it was full of beautiful things of the sky she stored there for them both, and because he could not see them and just laughed, there was no use for her on earth any more and she vanished." (pp. 143–45)

Inside Out—Outside In

THE ARROWMAKER AND THE CHILD

I

N. Scott Momaday, the Pulitzer-Prize-winning Kiowa author, has written and lectured extensively on the preeminence of language in our experience of being human. His sheer respect for language is epitomized by his well-known, life-long fascination with the story of the arrowmaker, out of his own Kiowa heritage:

If an arrow is well made, it will have tooth marks upon it. That is how you know. The Kiowas made fine arrows and straightened them in their teeth. Then they drew them to the bow to see that they were straight. Once there was a man and his wife. They were alone at night in their tipi. By the light of a fire, the man was making arrows. After a while he caught sight of something. There was a small opening in the tipi where two hides had been sewn together. Someone was there on the outside, looking in. The man went on with his work, but he said to his wife: "Someone is standing outside. Do not be afraid. Let us talk easily, as of ordinary things." He took up an arrow and straightened it in his teeth: then, as it was right for him to do, he drew it to the bow and took aim, first in this direction and then in that. And all the while he was talking, as if to his wife. But this is how he spoke: "I know that you are there on the outside, for I can feel your eyes upon me. If you are a Kiowa, you will understand what I am saying, and you will speak your name." But there was no answer, and the man went on in the same way, pointing the arrow all around. At last his aim fell upon the place where his enemy stood, and he let go of the string. The arrow went straight to the enemy's heart.

Momaday says about this story: "I have lived with the Kiowa story of the arrowmaker all my life. I have literally no memory that is older than that of hearing my father tell it to me when I was a small child" (Momaday, p. 11). He used this story as the first part of Section XIII of *The Way to Rainy Mountain,* his extended prose-poem in honor of his Kiowa ancestors and kins-people, and retells it and ponders its richness in a variety of places, including his moving, recent essay: "The Native Voice."

"The point of the story," Momaday says, "lies not so much in what the arrowmaker does, but in what he says—and indeed that he says it" (Momaday, p. 12). "The arrowmaker," he goes on to say, "is preeminently the man made of words. He has consummate being in language; it is the world of his origin and of his posterity, and there is no other." (Momaday, p. 18)

To be sure the arrowmaker story is about the power of skillful language craft, as well as arrow craft. But some readers have questioned the focus on killing the enemy which is central to what the arrowmaker does. The story is so definitive about the test of the man outside. Is the old Kiowa world of which the story is an expression so constructed that there can be no doubt as to this man's identity as an enemy? What else might he be?

These questions make explicit that there is a need now for stories that tell of those crucial events wherein a man might go beyond the patterns of warrior identity. Laurens van der Post's stirring volume, *A Bar of Shadow*, is one of the few books out of the post-World-War-II era which presents a believable picture of warriors from opposing sides actually transcending the whole experience of "the enemy," but the realities of life in the concentration camps, torture chambers, or just plain old poverties and luxuries of the twentieth century have done little to promote this sort of thinking.

I wondered: Are there Native American stories that explore the possibilities for transcending the terms of life as a warrior, stories wherein the need to identify and destroy enemies is not celebrated? What about stories that focus on the conditions under which a person realizes the wastefulness and destruciveness of warrior life, and makes a conscious decision not to pursue it? Surely stories like that exist. Why have they not been more popular, more well known? Is the seeming lack of such stories one more expression of the bias in the ways those trained in Western stories (the *Iliad* to *Star Wars*) attend to the literatures of other peoples, especially to oral-tradition literatures? Are we, collectively, overly attentive to stories of conflict, like zoologists focussing on the aggressive, competitive behavior of the dominant males rather than on the lines of relation and cooperation within, say, families of gorillas or musk-ox?

I came across "Smoking-Star, A Blackfoot Shaman," just such a story as I had been hoping for. A little more than halfway through Smoking Star's story the following episode is recorded:

About this time two things happened to me that turned my mind from war. Our chief led a party against the Cree and invited me to go. . . . When we reached the Cree country I was ordered out as a scout. It was dark. As I went along I saw a tepee all by itself. I went up to it quietly and looked in. There was no one in the tepee except a man, his wife, and a little child. The little child could just walk and was amusing itself by dipping soup from the kettle with a small horn spoon. The man and his wife were busy talking and paid no attention to the child. Now the child looked up and saw me peeping through the hole, toddled over to the kettle, dipped up some soup in the spoon and held it to my lips. I drank and the child returned to the kettle for more. In this way the child fed me for many minutes. Then I went away. As I went along to my own party, I thought to myself, "I do not like to do this, but I must tell my party about this tepee. When they know of it, they will come and kill these people. This little child fed me even when I was spying upon them, and I do not like to have it killed. Well, perhaps I can save the child; but then it would be too bad for it to lose its parents. No, I do not see how I can save them, yet I cannot bear to have them killed." I sat down and thought it over. After a while, I went back to the tepee, went in, and sat down. While my host was preparing the pipe, the child began to feed me again with the spoon. After we had smoked, I talked to the man in the sign-language, told him all about it, how I had come as a scout to spy upon them, how I was about to bring my war party, but that they had been saved by the little child. Then I directed the man to go at once, leaving everything behind in the tepee.

The man was very thankful and offered to give me a medicine bundle and a suit of clothes; but I refused, because I knew that my party would suspect me. Then the man suggested that he might place the bundle near the door, behind the bedding, so that when the war party came up and dashed upon the tepee, I would be the first to capture the bundle. . . .

Then I reported to my chief, telling him that I had discovered a camp of the enemy, but that I had not been up to it or seen anyone. He started out at once, all of us following. When we had surrounded the tepee, we gave a whoop and rushed upon it. I kept behind and while the others were busy counting coup upon the things in the back of the tepee, I seized the bundle by the door. The chief was angry, but said nothing. When we were again in camp, old Medicine-bear began to unwrap his war medicine-pipe to make a thank offering for our success. Then the chief faced me and denounced me as a traitor, accused me of warning the enemy and secreting the medicine bundle. My anger rose, I drew my knife, but at that moment old Medicine-bear sprang between us, holding the holy pipe in both hands. This is the custom, no one can fight over a holy pipe. The shaman made us each take the pipe and vow to put away our anger and hold our silence. So it was. Never have I forgotten that little child. Some great power was guarding it. Its medicine was strong. Many times have I prayed to that power and sometimes it helped me, but I do not yet know what power it is. Yet somehow I took little interest in war, the child's medicine did that to me. (Parsons, pp. 55–56)

Here is a story from a tribe (the Blackfeet) just as committed to warrior activity as the Kiowa, and not so far distant in space, for the Kiowa had migrated south from the Yellowstone country, home to traditional Blackfeet enemies, the Crow. Here is the familiar setting: the family in their tepee with an enemy peering through a hole in the skin covering. Except that the focus is different, for in this story we are with the raiding warrior on the outside looking in instead of inside feeling his eyes upon us, and the chief actor in the story is not one of the male warriors, but a child playing with a horn spoon in a soup kettle. And the key to survival lies not in the skillful handling of the potency of language, but in a gesture of daily life. We do not know if this child who can "just walk" is male or female, and it does not matter. The silent act of being fed by it from the family soup kettle reaches on through this warrior's intentions to that place in him where his own child-self resides.

This is the kind of story, I believe, that those who have resisted the story of the arrowmaker, with its wonderful presentation of the ingenious use of language to defend family and home, are looking for. This warrior, Smoking-Star, is brought into the enemy family itself by this simple act of being fed, which is not dependent on words. Language between the child and the warrior would not make a difference, even if they spoke the same one. It is the direct purity of the child's act, without language and seemingly without thought, that goes in so deep. The very silence of the act is its most powerful voice. In this story with its focus on the primal power of action to reach deep in, to bring about radical change in the human spirit, one is reminded of Goethe's Faust at the moment when he sits down at his desk to rewrite the opening lines of the Gospel of John,

"It is written: In the beginning was the word."
Here I am stuck at once. Who will help me on?
I am unable to grant the Word such merit,
I must translate it differently
If I am truly enlightened by the spirit.
"It is written: In the beginning was the Mind."
But why should my pen scour
So quickly ahead? Consider that first line well.
Is it the Mind that effects and creates all things?

It should read: "In the beginning was the Power."
Yet, even as I am changing what I have writ,
Something warns me not to abide by it.
The spirit prompts me, I see in a flash, what I need,
And write; "In the beginning was the Deed."
(Goethe, p. 44)

This is not to argue against the potency of human language. It is, however, to remind us of the limits of that potency, to lay alongside it elemental human action in its own
potency. The child in its singular play silently seeks out this
perhaps uncle, and seals his lips with a ladleful of soup, an act
which is repeated for "many minutes." The silence here is just
as telling as in the arrowmaker story, for it is the silence of
knowledge that the child in its play is right and powerful. It
has figured nothing out — that is a part of its power. It is there
like a chokecherry tree or a star. And this warrior finds his
whole life thrown suddenly into stark relief by this gesture —
the ladle proffered to him through the gap in the hides. He
takes part, he opens his lips, the soup pours into his mouth,
belly, brain, spirit. And war becomes of "little interest" to
him.

Does the difference between these two stories tell us anything about the two cultures from which they emerge, or are
such differences present in all societies and dependent on the
personalities of particular storytellers, or stories, or of particular historical circumstances? The way the two stories cor-
respond to each other is striking — are they in fact corollaries
of each other? Either story without the other seems to be only
part of a story; i.e., they seem to belong to a same story structure. The Kiowa story is the inside of the Blackfeet story.
Smoking-Star's story is the outside of the arrowmaker story.
Together they suggest a larger, more complete story. One
story needs the other, fundamentally, in order that the fullness

of a warrior's life be told and comprehended. The more such connected but discrete stories are permitted to rub up against each other, like ponies in a wild herd, the more understanding will be released.

The arrowmaker is as fine a human being as can be imagined, handling language, life, and death with all the dexterity human craftsmanship can muster. The child with his ladleful of soup is something else — perhaps a channel for understandings that transcend adult human structures and patterns. The child is, I suppose, the playful, the innocent, the lonely, and the nurturing mother all in one.

II

There is, however, a problem with the story of Smoking-Star. It was published by a white anthropologist, Clark Wissler, as a "created" story containing his knowledge of Blackfeet culture for a volume called *American Indian Life*, edited by Elsie Clews Parsons and published in 1922. Chagrined that I'd remembered a tale whose authenticity was suspect, I decided to ask Blackfeet people what they thought of the story. Could it have been like this for a Blackfeet warrior? Was it credible that a young warrior would be so moved by a child, and allow his enemies to escape? Was there anything in Blackfeet oral tradition that was similar? Or did it sound as if Wissler had imposed too much of his own culture's perspective onto what knowledge of Blackfeet culture he did in fact have? Had Wissler subtly Christianized the Blackfeet through his way of telling this story? I wrote to John "Buster" Yellow Kidney, an older Blackfeet man whom I knew and trusted. I sent a copy of the story along with my questions as to how trustworthy an account of it was of what actually could have happened in Blackfeet culture. I received the following notecard in reply:

Dear Roger,

I have heard the story you sent to me. It was told to me in that way by my Grandfather Yellow Kidney.

Buster

Many more questions leapt in my mind: How had Clark Wissler come into possession of this story? Why did he represent it as his own creation rather than from the Blackfeet oral tradition? Was there any possibility that it had been created by Wissler and then had somehow circled back into the Blackfeet oral tradition? What were the circumstances under which John Yellow Kidney had heard this story from his grandfather? What was the purpose or meaning of Grandfather Yellow Kidney's telling of it, as Buster understood that? Was it explicitly a teaching story about the limits of being a warrior? About attending to the seemingly insignificant?

Three weeks after the beginning of Operation Desert Storm, John Yellow Kidney came to the university to give a lecture on American Indian perspectives on world peace, and to give a pipe ceremony for American Indian soldiers in the Persian Gulf. We had a chance to talk over the story of Smoking-Star and my questions about it. He said that he was told this story by his grandfather in the late 1930s, along with his two older brothers, who later were in World War II. He thought the story came from an actual historical event two to three generations before his grandfather's time. There was even a man named for that story — Looking For Smoke — *his* father liked the story so much. And then he told another story:

A party of eleven Blackfeet warriors set out on a raid. One went back early, realizing that something bad was going to happen. Nine were wiped out by a Sioux party they ran into; one hid up under an embankment with lots of roots hanging down. One of the Sioux warriors went walking up through there, past all the dead, scalped, stripped bodies, looking for something on past them. He came along to where the young Blackfeet was hiding up under the embankment. As he neared, the eyes of the two men met — locked on each other — and they both recognized it. But the Sioux warrior kept on walking, as if he had not looked into the eyes of the other. After he left, the Blackfeet brave headed back home. On his way, he ran into the one who'd left before the fight. He said he'd seen the other nine come through where he was, their spirits, but not this one. They'd come through as flying swans, except they'd had the heads of the nine men who'd been killed. So he wondered about this one who was still alive.

This happened in the last generation of raiding between the tribes. Some time after the raiding stopped, there was a gathering of the various tribes who had formerly been enemies. It lasted a week, maybe more. An older Sioux man there told the story of walking on by the man hidden up under the bank after their eyes had met. He explained that he'd had an only son, a fine young man, who'd been killed on a raid. It had hurt him deeply inside. When his eyes met the eyes of the young man up under the embankment he had thought to himself, "Perhaps this young man is an only son of someone. If I kill him, others may feel the pain and sadness I feel for my dead son. I'll walk on by. I'll pretend that our eyes did not meet. That is what I did," he said. "Is that young man alive, and old now?" A man at the gathering stood up and said that he was the young man who had hidden up under the embankment with roots hanging down. They acknowledged each other and went back to one of their tipis; they adopted each other and spent much time together before the gathering broke up.

Buster ended by saying this was another story like the one of the child with the soup ladle. He thought that there were many such stories that exist in every tribe. Men who saw things in this way became healers and advisers, men of peace.

And so, my questions about Smoking-Star were answered by a story, as is only fitting. I do not know the other stories like these, but I do know that today we need them as much as we ever did: to be able to look directly into the eyes of "the enemy" and to discern there a person, like us, who is simply hungry or afraid, or someone's beloved son.

Trud

A COMIC OPERA WITH BLOAT,
(A VOICE FROM WITHIN, OR BELOW)

For Vera Mary Dunsmore, November 26, 1912–March 17, 1987 and Baptise La Moose, last of the Salish Dog Dancers.

One still must have chaos in oneself to be able to give birth to
     a dancing star.[a]
. . . a remark on the indignity of any closed system.[b]

TRUD
The Glutton. Throat. All throat.

[Throat, Indo-European base,
trud, stretched or swollen,
strumma, stiff.]

The road of the swollen throat,

Trud's road.

What does he eat?

Trud, he eats everything,
eats our desire.

"Finger lickin' good," he says.

Everything eats everything.

" . . . energy is the 'currency' of the 'economy' of nature,
the coin of the realm'
in the biotic community,

and . . . energy is transferred

by what ecologists
euphemistically
call phagic or trophic
relations

(more bluntly,
by one thing

EATING
another)."[c]

During the rite of initiation, the clowns are daubed with a
mixture of herbs and white chalk. At a given moment, an
elder, taking part in the ceremony, urinates in a vessel,
mixing his urine with the medicine. Another throws in snot
from his nose, while a Koshari woman pulls out some of
her pubic hair and adds it to the mixture. When all of these
ingredients have been well mixed, the chief takes some of
the medicine into his mouth and spits on the other Koshari.
The initiates do the same, and finally everyone drinks of
the medicine from a shell. Having drunk four times of the
medicine, they become fully-initiated Koshari.[d]

BLOAT.
Gee, Trud, don't people get mad? I mean, the white people.
Don't they think it's bad?

TRUD.

Sure. They get bent out of shape. Even invented a Religious Crimes Code to make it all illegal. But that's mostly sour grapes. The white people did the same thing, early on.

BL.

Did the same thing? What do you mean?

TR.

Saw the new life coming green out of plants in the spring rains. Saw the magic contained in seeds, new sprouts coming up into the light, winds and clouds bringing ocean to the mountains, the water. Saw that made food for us, for birds, animals, everything. And wanted that in their own lives, tried to get ahold of it.

BL.

How'd they try to get it?

TR.

With nails.

BL.

Nails?

TR.

Yeah. Nailed a guy to a tree like a bloody fruit seed. Tried to nail meat onto plants up on this hill. Said he came back up out of the ground like a sprouted seed. Then started drinking his blood and eating his meat like it was vegetables or something. Called him a god, but they were just trying to nail human onto plant so we wouldn't have to die, but could sprout up again after the spring rains; seed magic.

BL.

Did it work? Did they get human life nailed into that new life coming up out of the plants?

TR.

I don't think so. They started hating everybody who didn't think like them. But there were some gypsies up there on that hill. They were starving, destitute. The nails were made out of silver. One of those gypsies stole a couple—moonlight silver in his eyes: two less nails to be driven in. It's been okay for gypsies to steal ever since. Christians don't understand that. But early on they had their own clowns and gypsies too.

BL.

Really?

TR.

Yeah. Called them fools. One guy name of Symeon of Emesa, about five hundred years after the guy nailed to the tree — place called Turkey. He started out as a "Boskoi," one of the "browsers" or grass-eaters who lived in the open air, naked among herds of antelope. When he decided to become a clown, he walked into the city with a dead dog he'd found on the rubbish heap tied into his belt. There was a school near by and the kids began to shout, "Hey, a mad monk." On Sunday he took some walnuts and went into the church, cracking them and putting out the lamps. When they tried to drive him off, he climbed up into the pulpit and pelted the women with walnuts. They finally got him out, but on the way he kicked over the stalls of the pastry sellers, who beat him so bad he nearly died. After that, he dressed as a monk and flouted church rules by eating meat in public during Holy Week. He hopped and jumped in the streets, tripping people and pretending to be an epileptic. When John the Deacon suggested they go to the public baths, he said with a laugh, "Yes, let's go, let's go." Then stripped off his clothes in the street, wrapped them around his head like a turban, and rushed straight into the women's part of the baths. He mocked their attempts to turn religious life into a set of rules or respectable morals.[c]

BL.

Whew. He sounds as good as that gypsy with silver in his eyes.

TR.

Yeah. But they made him illegal too, after he died.

BL.

Why?

TR.

Too many others took it up, and they just had no way to control it, so they outlawed it.

The divine laws condemn those who practice folly after the manner of the great Symeon . . . and today such things are altogether forbidden (Nikon of the Black Mountains, eleventh century).[e]

But it was hard to stop. The church even had their Feast of Fools right after Christmas for centuries.

BL.

What was it like, Trud?

TR.

Well, on the Day of Circumcision

BL.

Ouch.

TR.

Yeah. January first, at the moment in the liturgy when they sang the words "He has put down the mighty from their seats and has exalted the humble and the meek," all the young guys in the clergy jumped up and drove the bishop and his assistants out. Then they put on masks, dressed as clowns, brought out wine and food, turned the altar into a feast table, elected a boy bishop, and shouted an obscene parody of the Holy Mass, a devil's mass. Sometimes a braying ass was brought right into the church and worshipped as the Lord of Disorder. This went on until the day of Epiphany.[f]

BL.

What'd you suppose it meant, Trud?

TR.

Don't know. Maybe just the other-side, knowing the other side is always there.

BL.

The other side?

TR.

Yeah. The other side of anything, everything. It's always there and it always matters. And we know it. We just don't like to admit it. Humans at their best have always found ways to let it in, give it its place in their little schemes. Usually some clown — fool — madman has had to do it.

But there is something that no order can ban, regardless of all restrictions: . . . The awareness that there exists an outside, an unprotected, insecure, untested otherness which . . . makes it impossible to maintain the absolute and infinite validity of the accepted order . . . is not the clown perhaps himself the laughter of the Infinite about the Finite when it pretends to be absolute? . . . That God should laugh about the order which its inventors, maintainers and utilizers attribute to his holy will, this is worse than blasphemy. . . . This is why a suppression of the clown will be attempted again and again. But it will never succeed.[f]

BL.
Do you believe that Trud, that they'll never succeed in suppressing the clowns? Remember what they did to the old singers and storytellers of the Ukraine — invited them to a big conference from all over Russia, the oral history of a people, and killed every last one — wiped out overnight.
TR.
But it's still going. Didn't you see that Ukrainian guy playing Bach's fifth organ fugue like a madman on his accordion last week? That's part of it. It finds a way to go on. Its strength is very subterranean, very snake. Look at the Turk.
BL.
The Turk?
TR.
Yeah. You know — the guy who was born out of whack — with his intestinal tract in backwards, reversed.
BL.
Backwards?

TR.

Yeah. Eats with his ass and shits out his mouth.

BL.

Whew. Guess who's coming to dinner?

TR.

Yep. You always know when the Turk's coming to eat because there will be a paper plate out on the table amongst the china ones.

BL.

A paper plate?

TR.

Yep. The Turk has to take his pants down and sit on his plate in order to eat. He broke lots of china ones sitting on them so now they use paper plates.

BL.

Why do they call him the Turk? Was he a boskoi?

TR.

I don't know.

BL.

Are you one too? A Turk, I mean. Sounds sort of close to Trud.

TR.

Yeah. Maybe we're cousins. At least my intestines ain't in in reverse.

BL.

But it's stories like that that'll get those clowns suppressed. They're pretty extreme.

TR.

Yep. Gotta be. They're supposed to explore everything. No sacred cows or chiefs either. They have to go inside, underneath, around back, turn it all upside down, inside out, backwards, nowards — to find out, or just to keep things flexible. Otherwise stuff gets brittle and stale. Besides, human beings are very extreme, we need some extreme clowns.

BL.

What do you mean, we're very extreme?

TR.

We'll go to any lengths to get what we want. Any lengths. The
clowns hold that up to us like a mirror. One time,

> one of the Hopi clowns lassoed a large white mastiff and
> another . . . clown beat it to death slowly, with a stone. He
> sat astride of the wretched cur after the rope had nearly
> choked it, and then he beat on its head with a stone. Jose,
> who did the killing, cut off the dog's head and made a
> longitudinal incision down its belly. Two of them pulled
> out the guts, pluck, etc. They then threw one of their num-
> bers down and thrust the clotted dog's blood in his mouth.
> They rubbed each other's faces thoroughly and roughly
> with the blood. One of the four of them got an old frag-
> ment of blue mantle and with the dog's guts girdled it
> around him. He took the dog's head in his hands and
> chased the others. When he overtook them or struck them
> with the dog's head, they fell down as if dead, but presently
> got up again. There was much play in this case.[g]

BL.

God, Trud. I don't think I like that.

TR.

Maybe not. But remember what Talayesva said when a white
school principal frowned at the clown's sexual play:

> We called off the demonstration, led the old Katcina to our
> "house," gave her some corn meal, and told her to take our
> prayers to the Six-Point-Cloud People. She seemed very
> pleased and said, "All right, your reward shall be rain."

> Then I turned to my partners and said, "I'm going to fix
> that white man." I walked up to him, shook hands, and
> said in Hopi, "Well white man, you want to see what goes

on, don't you? You have spoiled our prayers, and it may not rain. You think this business is vulgar, but it means something sacred to us. This old Katcina is impersonating the Corn Maiden: . . . we must have intercourse with her so that our corn will increase and our people will live in plenty. If this were evil, we would not be doing it. You are supposed to be an educated man, but you had better go back to school and learn something more about Hopi life." He seemed embarrassed, reached into his pocket, drew out a half-dollar, and said, "Here, take this and get some tobacco." I thanked him and sent a man after the tobacco.[h]

I think the killing of the dog is something like the sex, something they have to do. Death's part of it too — the whole fertility cycle.
BL.
But smashing its head in with a stone after it's been caught with a rope? It doesn't have a chance. Reminds me of a story I heard from a woman up north, one of those cold mountain tribes.

I seen the cops catch a wild dog that had strayed too close to town and had killed a couple dogs. . . . They took the dog on the other side [of the street] and tied him up. They then came back on this side and start shooting at him. It must have been about 30 yards. I was about seven and counted the shots. Thirteen times, they shot him. The first time he let out a big yelp, then he seemed to know they weren't going to stop, so he'd just grunt a little every time another bullet would hit. After they finished shooting at him, they drug him away. He wasn't dead. His back was broke about three places and his legs, everything. He didn't seem to have a will but I felt then that he was still proud.

That was the first lesson I got in human dignity. I often

thought about it after that (it was the first time I'd seen anything get killed outside insects). I wondered why they didn't put a gun to his head, and pull the trigger once, letting him die in dignity, and leaving themselves some too.[i]

Trud, what makes that clown smashing in that dog's head with a stone any different than those cops?

TR.

You're right, Bloat, to be asking that. I'm not sure, but I think it has something to do with the fact that the cops don't have any reason, any purpose for doing it. They just do it because they enjoy it.

BL.

Enjoy it? Enjoy what?

TR.

Enjoy inflicting pain, like on that wild dog. It makes them feel powerful. And they can fill their emptiness for awhile with that feeling.

BL.

Isn't that what those clowns are doing too — just destroying that dog's life with a stone?

TR.

I don't think so, Bloat. The duty of those clowns is to teach and to heal, so they've got a purpose, and they're trained. They want us to understand how much we are in love with the feeling destroying gives us, and how far we'll go to get what we want. They want to show us how dangerous that is. Look at this from last month's paper. Yep, May, 1987.

The Honduran government just announced that it's tightening up its adoption policies for obtaining Honduran children. They discovered people from the U.S. were adopting the Honduran kids, bringing them back up here and selling their body parts to our organ banks.[i]

Now that's extreme. But there's something else, Bloat. They want us to know that death's a part of it too, part of the big cycles. The seed in the ground dies to germinate. The soil itself, all that debris the plants grow in, it's all the broken down pieces of the bodies of everything that ever lived here, or got blown here. Every mouthful we take, Bloat, is someone's, something's, life. And we better know that, and live like we know it. They sacrifice the dog's life so we'll begin to know some of this, and a lot more I don't understand. Sacrifice, that means to make sacred. The cops just want the thrill of watching the bullets from their hand guns explode the dog's body. They don't understand that that explosion takes place inside themselves, too, and in the heart of the child. And they'd never actually get down into that dog's body, eat its blood and wrap themselves in its guts. The clowns go down into it, inside it — they are that smashed-in dog, we all are — guts wrapped around other bodies. The cops keep it nice and safe and distant, all tied up, touching it only with their high-speed pieces of metal.

BL.

Gee, Trud, maybe so. Maybe the dog's life can be sacrificed for all that. . . . But I don't accept it. Maybe I'm just too protected or something, but those "browsers" or "boskois" out grazing with the herds of antelope — they seem so calm, and they are not ignorant about death. What about that dog? What about its life? What does it think and feel? What would it say, if we listened to it? Wouldn't it ask for mercy? Ask that they find another way to teach us? Doesn't everything that ever gets sacrificed want to live too? Did those clowns really care about that dog's life?

TR.

Maybe, Bloat. It's always said about those clowns that "they know something about themselves," something the cops don't know.

BL.

What do they know about themselves, the clowns, Trud? Is it like what the boski know?

TR.

It's not for me to say, Bloat. I can only guess.

> Men . . . are poorer than the beasts . . . for each creature has a special gift of strength or sagacity, while to men has been given only the power of guessing.[k]

But I don't think it's any accident that Hopi clowns make a house of ashes in the plaza, or that their smile, the circles under their eyes, are painted with ashes and soot. The backwards people among the O'odham are even called Ashes.

BL.

Why, Trud?

TR.

How should I know? Maybe they know they're the same as that dog, that they've got this form, this meat, this blood for awhile, and then they'll go on to the other world too? Maybe they think that their flesh and the dog's flesh really aren't that different — that this body is a house of ashes.

BL.

Trud, it scares me. Aren't you willing to accept that killing just because it's a dog's life that's being destroyed, and not because it's the clowns doing it? Does all the ritual, all the ceremony, all the good reasons for the sacrifice make the dog's life less valuable or its death less painful? Just because we humans can be cruel and brutal and uncaring, what gives the clowns the right to show that at the cost of the dog's life? Maybe the fool is different than the clown. Maybe the fool never presumes he knows enough about himself or this universe to be able to kill like that. Maybe that's why those "browsers" lived naked among the antelope. There's something in those clowns that's scary.

TR.

But you have to eat.

BL.

Yes. But killing that dog isn't for eating. It might be for celebrating the cycles of life and death in eating, but that's abstract. I wouldn't kill for that.

TR.

Look at the Katsinas. They say they're the ones who've gone on. That they're the world of nature from way before there were any humans — the forms of beauty and growth working together at this world.

BL.

Trud?

TR.

Yeah?

BL.

When we die, when I die, what happens to us?

TR.

Think about those clowns, Bloat. They're naked. They know enough to remain naked. And when he steals from you, you consider yourself blessed. A clown owns nothing except his nakedness, which is why his breech clout may be snatched from him at any moment in the plaza:

Nogwo-dho-
(*Naked*)

I don't know Bloat — that "something" the clown knows about himself — some say that he knows evil — that it's bound up with good, here on this fertile earth, at least for us —

Evil can be overcome by man only through knowledge, the
knowledge of evil; and it seems . . . that man can know a
thing, as man, only through participation . . . good and evil

Trud 146 | 147

are, here on earth, inextricably bound up together. This is to us the great mystery of life on earth.[1]

I've heard the old men say, Bloat, that the reason we need a tree there in the center to pray for us is because it's innocent, in a way we just can't be, because we're human, and so the prayers of the tree can get through when ours can't. I guess the clowns are standing in all this, and they know that fertility is the biggest power.

BL.

Fertility?

TR.

Yeah. The ability of the universe to reproduce itself. It's in everything. The way bees and small insects crawl way down into the sex organs of plants to eat, and carry little pieces of plant sex away on their hairy legs and take it to other plants to make them fertile, make their seeds grow. Whatever death is, Bloat, we're part of this universe that keeps being born and just goes on and on and won't end anywhere. Can't. All time and all space can't keep up with it. They're just ideas we use to try to pretend we know where we're at.

> The heart of the Hopi concept of clowning is that we are all clowns. . . . We are going to clown our way through life making believe that we know everything and when the time comes, possibly no one will be prepared after all to enter the next world.[m]

Look at this stuff, Bloat, this dirt and sticks and stones and stuff. It's not dead or alive. It's this vast, endless process of going on. . . . We're part of it too. All we can do is sing our part in it, tell stories, dance.

> I have seen one of them gather about him his melons, green and ripe, raw peppers, bits of stick and refuse, unmention-

able water, live puppies — or dead, no matter — peaches, stones and all, in fact everything soft enough to be forced down his gullet, including wood ashes and pebbles, and with the greatest apparent gusto, consume them all at a single sitting. Once after such a repast, two of these Ne-we pretended, though their stomachs were bloated to distortion, to still be hungry. They fixed their staring eyes on me, and motioned me to give them something else to eat! I pitied them profoundly, but as it is considered the height of indecency to refuse a Ne-we anything, I ran home, caught up some crackers, threw them into a paper, and in order to make them relish the better, poured a pint or two of molasses over them. I wrapped an old woolen army jacket around this as a present to the enterprising clowns, and hurried back. They were anxiously waiting — the people watching them to see how much more they could get away with. I cast the bundle into the plaza. The two immediately fell to fighting for its possession, consequently broke the paper, scattered some of the crackers about the ground and daubed the back of the coat thoroughly with the molasses. They gathered up the fragments of crackers and ate them, with their whole burden of adhesions, then fought over the paper and ate that, finally tore pieces out of the back of the coat with their teeth and ate them (though it nearly choked them to do so), after which the victor put the coat on and triumphantly wore it, his painted skin showing like white patches through the holes he had bitten in the back of the coat.[n]

BL.
Trud, I've been thinking about the Turk.
TR.
What about him?
BL.
It's a good thing he was born with his mouth in the right place.

Otherwise that thing would've emptied into his brain. You know where the acupuncture point is for hemorrhoids?

BL.

No. Where is it?

BL.

Right up on top of your head, where the soft spot is in babies. Trud?

TR.

Yeah?

BL.

Do you suppose we were open at both ends way back in the beginning? Stuff just gushing right on through?

TR.

Gawd, Bloat, I don't know.

BL.

If we were, I wonder how we got one end closed off and moved down the side to where the mouth is?

TR.

Yeah. And how'd we grow teeth? And that tongue. Was it just an extra finger with no bones banging on the side of our head, like it does now in our mouths?

BL.

Will we ever know, Trud?

TR.

Think about the Turk, Bloat. Does he worry about having his ass where everybody's mouth is, and vice versa? Nope. He just takes down his pants and sits on a plate of food. He has the best time he can. You know, I was sitting on the hill watching the sky the other night, and there were some medium-sized clouds hanging over the hills south of here, seemed like beings of some kind. They caused me to wonder. We don't know what we are, Bloat, don't know what anything else is either, just some creatures moving around on this planet somewhere in space. We don't know what all this is. But we know we have to name it — and we know we need to take part in it, find our place in it, best we can. It's mighty powerful, Bloat. The clowns know that and open up to it, open the whole people up. That's why they'll never stop them.

To us a clown is somebody sacred, funny, powerful, ridiculous, holy, shameful, visionary. He is all this and then some more. Fooling around, a clown is really performing a spiritual ceremony. He has a power. It comes from the thunder beings, not the animals or the earth. In our Indian belief a clown has more power than the atom bomb. This power could blow the dome off of the capitol.°

BL.
How can a clown have more power than the atom bomb?
TR.
I know that sounds unbelievable. When I first read Lame Deer's statement, I thought he was just being himself, old John Fire, you know, exaggerating everything for effect. I remember thinking, Come on, John Fire. I know those clowns are really something, but more powerful than atom bombs? I should have known. I should have known to take his statement as literally true, and I should have known it was understated. He just picked the handiest thing most of us would be impressed by as having lots of power. The atom bomb ain't even close. The clown is the closest we'll ever get Bloat, to the universe itself, being it. They're all of it; laughter and shit, sperm and the whip, rain and piss, all of nuclear and astrophysics in one ridiculous body. He's the contradiction in everything. He has to violate every taboo, everything sacred, in order to show its other side, to keep it living. That's his duty. He's the black holes in space, and the space the black holes are in. He's the black holes turned inside out, upside down, backwards to the furthest edge of the universe we'll ever know — inside us too, and we know it, and we know it in laughter.

BL.

What the hell is laughter, Trud?

TR.

Some say it's convulsions. It's no accident Symeon ran around the streets of Emesa like an epileptic tripping people up. It's convulsions, like orgasm or grief.[p] Seizes us and opens us to the bigger cycles where chaos and death are fertility. Keeping the order, keeping it open to cycles that give birth to stars and corn—the clown's duty is to be that opening out onto the thunder beings. Our moral orders are part of the "place" we make for ourselves in this vast plane of earth and sky, but they've got limits. The Christians closed off their own order from the bigger one and then absoluteized it. Evil, death, and chaos were out. Outside. And once they'd made their own moral order absolute, cut off, a closed system, they had to create atom bombs. Lame Deer says, Bloat, that the clown's power comes from the thunder beings, not from earth or the animals.

> These thunderbirds are part of the great spirit. Theirs is about the greatest power in the whole universe. It is the power of the hot and cold clashing way above the clouds. It is lightning—blue lightning from the sun. It is like a colossal welding, like the making of another sun. It is like atomic power. The thunder power protects and destroys. It is good and bad, as God is good and bad, as nature is good and bad, as you and I are good and bad.[q]

And once a people cut themselves off from that power, Bloat, and make their own power absolute, they'll try to banish the clowns, like Louis the XIV did, for daring to ridicule Madame du Maintenon from the stage.[r] But Madame du Maintenon herself had created that ridicule, and she and Louis can no more stop it than they can stop snow from falling in December. It's simply the other side of what she herself is. Otherwise we get the closed system, the moral monster, the scarecrow.

Once we've cut off from the thunder beings we have to try to create them from within to lend power to our own absolute systems. And that is why, dear Bloat, there are jet fighters, all the time, in the skies over this city. They are the Religious Crimes Code in the sky.

BL.

Whew, Trud. All that makes my brain ache. Tell me another Turk story.

TR.

All right. Here's a short one. They say the greatest fear the young women have is when they're out on a blind date and they go to kiss him good night, they'll discover he's the Turk.

BL.

I'll bet they don't French him.

TR.

They can't. He won't let them.

BL.

He won't let them?

TR.

Nope. Tickles too much.

BL.

Trud, will you sleep next to me?

TR.

Sure.

BL.

Will you wake me up every half hour to make sure I don't go to sleep forever?

TR.

Yeah, I'll check on you.

BL.

Thanks. Good night, Trud.

TR.

Good night, Bloat.

BL.

Trud?

TR.

Yeah?

BL.

Why didn't they teach us this stuff in school?

TR.

They can't.

BL.

Why can't they?

TR.

They don't know it.

BL.

They don't?

TR.

Nope. They know other stuff that they think is more important.

BL.

What other stuff?

TR.

The skeptical position may be summed up in general by the statement: We can never know whether the universe is finite or infinite in space and time. The position that takes its guidance from the procedures and results of scientific inquiry may be summed up thus: We can never establish at any given time whether some account of the universe which happens to be preferred to other accounts proposed at the same time, will remain adequate in the face of continuing inquiry. It is most important to realize that these two positions are quite different and it is only a very crude interpretation which will cover both by the assertion that we shall never know the truth. For a skeptical view assumes that there is some structure possessed by the real universe, only men cannot hope to know it. For the scientifically guided view, however, there is no independent thing to which we can refer as "the universe" and with which various accounts may be matched in order to determine their relative truth. There is only, on the one side, a growing mass of observational data and, on the other, the variety of theoretic schemes for its interpretation. The assumption that there is a universe studied by cosmology which must already have one or the other of the properties, finitude or infinity, with respect to its spatial and temporal extent, needs to be challenged as not in fact required by the operative procedures of scientific cosmology.[s]

BL.
Gosh, Trud, is that really more important stuff?
TR.
You'll have to decide for yourself.
BL.
Oh. . . . Trud?
TR.
Yeah?
BL.
I want to change my name.
TR.
Change your name?
BL.
Yes. I want to be called Boskos, after those naked, grass-eating fools among the herds of antelope, the Boskoi.
TR.
You don't just go around changing your name, Bloat.
BL.
No. I'm serious, Trud. Help me.
TR.
What do you want me to do?
BL.
Nothing much. Just call me Boskos from now on, like that was my name forever, when you're talking to me — that's all.
TR.
Okay. Boskos. . . . Boskos! It sure ain't Bloat.

BOS.

Nope. You can call me Bosk for short.

TR.

Okay, Bosk. Good night.

BOS.

Good night, Trud. Trud?

TR.

Yeah.

BOS.

Thanks.

[They lie down next to each other under the stars.]

TR.

Yeah. Good night, Bosk.

[Bosk sleeps. Trud gets up, dances by himself with the night sky, the stars.]

APPENDIX

The Etymologies

Cosmos — world, universe, harmony.
    4. Any of a group of tall plants
    of the composite family
    with feathery leaves
    and white, pink, or purple flowers.
    (Plants having flower heads
    of a large number of small flowers
    in clusters surrounded by small leaves:
    daisy, aster, sunflower.)
Chaos — Greek, abyss chainenin, to gape.
    (the "disorder" of formless matter
    and infinite space.)
cf. *chasm* — yawning, hollow, gulf.
    A deep crack
    in the earth's surface.

Splitting apart.
To gape — as in yawning
or hunger.
To stare with mouth open,
as in
wonder or surprise.
gape worm — a parasitic roundworm
   infesting the large
   respiratory passages
   of young poultry
   and causing
The Gapes.
   Gape — in zoology:
   the measure
   of the widest possible opening
   of a mouth
   or beak.
Primordial — primus, first, plus
   ordiri, to begin.
   from the beginning
   to come into being
Be — a defective verb.
   parts from
   stay, remain, linger,
   grow, become, occur
Hohokam — those who are gone.
be — Indo-European roots,
es — am, is
wes — stay
bheu — become
   a defective verb
Play — to take care of, be used to.
   Indo-European base — *hlgh* —
   to take up one's promise.
   to move lightly, rapidly

or erratically:
frisk, flutter,
as sunlight plays on waves —
colts or butterflies.
Movement,
especially when rapid, free,
or light.

The clowns place pinches of sand soaked with watery coffee from the pretend bladder of the woman clown (sweet
urine, they say) on the tongue of the little boy clown.
"Now you will have wisdom," they tell him. (Stephen, 366)

NOTE

These two characters, Trud and Bloat, began to speak in
me in the early morning, in Tucson, Arizona, the summer of
1987 as I worked with materials on the ritual clowns of the
Pueblo Indians.

Trud's voice is prior, is the voice which has "answers" to my
ponderings of the clowns. I had problems with his voice: it
knew more than it should/could, or had any right to know. It
needed to know it could be very wrong in its viewpoint. And
so, Bloat's voice emerged, never quite far enough, but just far
enough, I hope, to keep Trud's voice from becoming oppressive.

Trud's voice has lots of room in it for other voices, the
voices of those who, it appears to me, have spoken most
clearly about ritual clowns and clowning. And so whole undi-
gested chunks of other voices get dropped right on into Trud's
voice. These chunks are set off by italics.

The Etymologies represent another form through which to
approach some of the basic terms of the Trud-Bloat dialogue,
basic terms that enter into the prose of the "afterword" in a
significant way. Though derived wholly from the dictionary,
they are meant to be a poem, to these very words themselves

and in the language which seems furthest from poetry — the language of the lexicographer.

The "afterword" contains the parts or dimension of my own thoughts on ritual clowns that I saw no way to internalize in the Trud-Bloat dialogue, and yet these thoughts too, asked for a place. And so one October Sunday, sitting at the round, orange kitchen table with the Amazon parrots flying about in my friend's house, I committed them to paper.

AFTERWORD

Trud arose from my dissatisfaction with the responses to ritual clowning in the various journals of anthropology and literature. Most observers either tried to understand clowning from within a particular culture's present stated values or tried to interpret it in the light of imported conceptual matrixes such as psychoanalysis, Zen Buddhism, or the philosophy of laughter. Neither way felt right to me. While those working to understand from within particular cultures where clowning was observed (like Dr. Louis Hieb with his idea that the major function of Hopi clowning is that of "practical ethics") are to be commended for the respect and care with which they approached the respective culture, in the final analysis their approach seemed too cautious, or so at pains not to offend the origin communities where they'd witnessed the clowning, that they ignored or avoided larger, more obvious cosmic aspects of clowning, like the participation in cycles of fertility that go far beyond human moralities.

Hieb, interestingly enough, in his doctoral dissertation, suggests the significance of the cosmic dimension of ritual clowning, but as something which is past:

Conrad Hyers has recently written,
It is the special talent of the clown to return us to the paradise of innocence where there is neither good nor evil;

and the revel and permissiveness of the carnival becomes a symbolic, if not actual, repetition of that primordial chaos prior to the creation of the sacred cosmos.[t]

"Hopi clowns before the twentieth century appear to have done just that. They affirmed the sacred through a via nega-tive and were largely concerned with what Mary Douglas has called "the internal lines" of their society. In the context of rapid social-cultural change . . . the humor of the clowns has become . . . a means of confrontation and it is now the "external boundaries" which concern the clown . . . the task of the clown is to conform behavior . . . the emphasis is to be placed on practical ethics. . . . The clown performance consists . . . of a series of situations which are at odds with the [Hopi ethical] system . . . the ritual clowns portray those situations which represent life as it should not be."[u]

While I am not in a position to determine just how much Hopi (and other cultures') clowning has changed under the impact of the "rapid social-cultural change" of the last cen-tury or so, Trud proceeds from the assumption that the older function of the clown (the return to the paradise beyond good and evil, to the primordial chaos prior to the sacred cosmos) is still and always the deepest, most elemental function of the clown. This is where beauty and death have their twin do-main, for neither are to be domesticated by ethics, but take up their existence as wild elements of reality.

When we are given the quick answer to the question,

"What is that clown over there actually up to?"
"Oh, he's just keeping order."

the understanding of the answer has everything to do with what is meant by "order." To be sure, he is a keeper of the order of this particular ceremony at this particular time in the cycle of ceremonies, in this particular plaza, of these people, but he is also, simultaneously, a keeper of the primordial order in which the link between chaos and cosmos is necessary to there being any order at all.

Disharmony, imbalance in the cosmos, has to do at its most fundamental level with the attempt to deny, ignore, or block the primal connection to what we call chaos, to try to keep out and away whatever does not fit into our systems. That is the ultimate precariousness of "post-modern" technological, bureaucratic society. It fears this chaos/cosmos link, tries to deny it, and in the process paradoxically actually stimulates the disintegrating processes of acid rain, nuclear-environmental holocaust, and bacteriological (smallpox blanket) warfare. In a word, it stimulates the full pollution of the cosmos.

Trud is situated in the sort of understanding in which chaos and order are not opposites, but part of a single pattern or configuration, and one that is never static, always moving. What we call chaos is simply the breakdown of some established order with which we have identified our security, or the exploratory play at the heart of being seeking new pathways through which to express itself. That which is wild, playful, primal, does not lend itself (readily) to our categories and efforts to order. And so our fear. Order equals control. Chaos equals "other," an other which is experienced as strange, and somehow beyond us. Chaos is the house of fecundity, and vitality. All orders, no matter how necessary, rich and organic, must have porousness about them through which the energy of the chaotic may flow. Chaos actually may simply be those aspects of reality (which is infinite) which our finite systems and brains are inadequate to express or experience rationally. Chaos may simply be a category of the rational mind — including everything in it which is "other." The development of greater tolerance for what is labeled chaos is a social/historical necessity. And to learn to navigate where there is no system, improvisationally. And without the desire to bring what we experience on such journeys into any system. Chaos is womb, is void, is night, is the emptiness which is full of every possible thing, at the heart of the star-burst energy within everything.

The Navajos have over 350,000 conjugations of the verb "to go," according to Gary Witherspoon.[v] I believe this is because they realize that the energy of the universe lies in movement rather than in being; lies in the movement into being, the movement as being, the movement out of being, on into other forms. We tend to locate reality in particular beings that exist now, rather than in flows of energy along certain channels, like tribes, or species, which are always changing. The reason "to be" has to be an "imperfect" verb form is that it cannot adequately express the motion into and through and out of being that being is. "To be" tends toward existence as static. What we call chaos is whatever tends to disrupt the structures of "permanence" we try to erect. The finest human structures are those whose foundation and form are informed by impermanence, change, like the petroglyphs pecked into the patina on the red sandstone in the canyons of Arizona. They reveal the stone beneath the patina of coloration weathered onto it, and in that revealing express significant form — a wild goat, a herd of antelope, dancers, the moon, or a bird. They are for a time. They will weather in again. They can be renewed, as long as we care to, and have the will. They rely on the "permanence" of the rock, which is made of sand. They contain the color of blood, and of fire. Chaos is the mother, devouring and fecund, never to be ignored by any order. Trud arises from these. Trud overturns, teases, laughs, provokes. He will always try to see things backward and turned inside out because he knows all human orders have a tendency to rigidity, to the pretense of permanence or exclusiveness, or superiority. And he knows the orders of nature put our moralities and rationalities into the proper perspective because they contain what we call chaos as an essential ingredient.

The idea that the universe is rational, that there are rational laws to its structure which the mind of man can discover and be secure in and have control of, is an offense both to the richness and complexity of the universe and of the human mind. Dreams and seizures will always be necessary in order for us to know what we are in this world. The rational order of the universe is a useful idea, but limited. We tend to be highly selective, not only in what we remember, but in what we perceive. Our brains create rational structure in order to organize those aspects of reality that we need and want. We ignore the rest until it ceases to exist for us. Aldous Huxley's idea that the brain is a complex reducing valve because we couldn't survive the influx of it all, seems precise. The experience of chaos is often simply the experience that the order we've established has outlived its usefulness, or encountered events for which it was not structured, or grown feeble, or become ready to give way to an order that takes on a larger or more complex chunk of what is real.

Trud is not a celebration of chaos. Trud is a celebration of the necessity of the proper place of, and respect for, what we call chaos in any so-called order that wishes to survive. Perhaps Trud starts us thinking about chaos and its place. Where does it come from? What do we mean by it? How is it connected to cosmos? Why do we fear it? What are the myths of navigation regarding it? What's beyond the chaos/cosmos dialectic? Can one exist without the other?

There are many forms of beauty, but the most infinite one is the beauty of this necessary interplay between cosmos and chaos, whch is primordially the basis for everything. The beauty lies not only in the vastness and mysteriousness of the link, but in its necessity. To inhabit a cosmos that is divorced from chaos is to inhabit a lethal illusion, which is why children are important. The clown is primordial child, reminding us of our origin and destiny, and of the tentativeness of our orders. Through delight in play he overturns everything, and that overturning reveals and heals.

My concern in Trud is that we do not take up a position in

regards to these ritual clowns that is merely the inversion of the older Religious Crimes Code response. The Bureau of Indian Affairs perpetrators of the Religious Crimes Code were shocked by the public sexual play of the clowns, by the ingestion of urine and feces, human and otherwise. We, on the other hand, appear to have focused on the positive moral content of the ritual clowning (Hieb's "practical ethicism") while largely ignoring the cosmic dimension. If one stands in the overriding concern for fertility that informs the ceremonies of the clowns, then their mock copulations and excremental excursions are the communal participation in that most powerful of all mysteries — the capacity of the universe to reproduce itself, on and on forever. This happens to, in, and through us along with everything else, as our bodies mix with someone else's and go on in new form — the children. Eating, digestion, excretion, decay, growth — all are integral to this process of going on — and the clowns act out for us the great cosmic drama of reproduction.

They remind us that the smell of shit is closely linked to the smell of flowers and the taste of food; that dung is fertile; that urine is the body's rain, daily; and that to drink its "sweetness," to purify ourselves with it, is not gross, but is to partake of the great cycles of moisture around us and rolling through us, and not to turn away in fear or disgust from the moisture of our own bodies — to revel in it, to laugh at/with it, to honor through humor and games the ways we too stand in these great cycles of moisture, reproduction, decay, and excretion. Of these mysterious, wonderful processes that go beyond all morality, the clowns remind us.

TRUD.
The reason, dear Bosk, we have consigned the clown to his place among the animal cages and trapeze artists and shrieking children and obese idiots is that we fear him. We fear his nihilism. For like his consorts, beauty and death, he is not to

be domesticated. He is the perfect violator of every taboo. His "nature is not simply supernatural: it is the opposite of Nature. He is the anti-Natural God," he "shall be afraid of nothing, and [he] shall regard nothing as sacred. No place shall be forbidden to [him]." The circus clown of today is a mere memory of the clown as he appears in the plaza, today.[w]

BOSK.

And just what is this fear of nihilism all about, Trud?

TR.

It is, Bosk, I think, the fear that what we have put together as our lives, our societies, our histories, is bogus, is a lie, a shoddy job in the face of the vast, paradoxical mystery which life itself is. So we cling to what we have been able to cobble together and those who would point out to us the nails and seams of this old shoe, Western Civilization let us call it, must be nihilists, for they would leave us with nothing. This nothing we call our fear.

Unless we can conspire to be this emptiness inside ourselves that we fear and try to fill with every something, we never will be anything. Nothing is only the other side of every something. Which is why I suppose, dear Bosk, when Yahweh finally gave Moses his true name, he told him, simply, **i am** is my name forever.

And his wife is emptiness, nothing. And without her, he could not be. Whatever this one is, beyond all duality, even the duality of chaos and cosmos, emptiness is the road toward it.

> But one does not necessarily speak
> in order to be heard.
> It is sometimes enough
> that one places his voice
> on the silence,
> for that in itself
> is a whole and appropriate
> expression of one's spirit.[x]

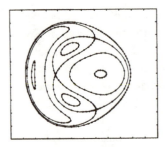

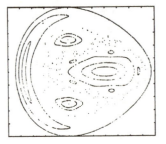

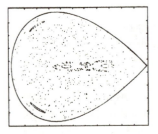

Star galactic orbital patterns from Chaos, *J. Gleick, p. 148. Reproduced by permission of* Astronomical Journal *and the author.*

Researchers in the new science of chaos imagine a wall at the edge of the galaxy. (In the Lakota world there is a real wall, of water, at the edge of the universe.) Stars orbiting the center of the galaxy on a time scale of hundreds of millions of years create donut-shaped patterns when they experimentally intersect this imagined wall. These patterns twist themselves into figure-eights, then move toward "chaos" when subjected to increased energy in the researcher's computer systems. (From another perspective, however, these patterns reveal a panda's face tipped on its right side, or a spirit mask carved by Kwaquital or Iroquois dreamers.) As researchers increase the energy in their systems to higher and higher levels, they report some star-orbits became "so unstable that the points" scattered "randomly across the paper. . . . The picture became quite dramatic: evidence of complete disorder mixed with the clear remnants of order, forming shapes that suggested islands and chains of islands . . ." (Gleick, 147). Or the panda-face-woodland-spirit-mask opens into a visual scream, or the face of a young woman in silent orgasm. In the researcher's last graphic, this mask/face elongates and its features disintegrate into particles of dust. Barely discernible within these dust particles, a tall dancer appears. Of course, the ancient/contemporary dreamers of Native America know this dancer in the cosmic dust at the edge of the galaxy. Perhaps it is the primordial bison bull holding back the wall of water that will sweep away the world at the end of this time. This knowledge is a manifestation of Earth's mind.

NOTES

a Nietzsche, F. *The Portable Nietzsche.* "Prologue" to *Zarathustra,* Section 5. New York: Viking, 1954, p. 129.

b Babcock, B. A. "Arrange Me into Disorder: Fragments and Reflections on Ritual Clowning," in John MacAloon, ed., *Rite, Drama, Festival, Spectacles: Rehearsals Toward a Theory of Cultural Performance.* ISHI Press, 1984, p. 103. (I am especially indebted to Dr. Babcock's work. She pointed to several central sources for this piece, as well as encouraging, through her examples, using a form more appropriate to the subject than the scholarly essay.)

c Callicott, J. B. "The Search for an Environmental Ethic," in *Matters of Life and Death: New Introductory Essays in Moral Philosophy,* 2nd ed., ed. Tom Regan. Random House, 1986, p. 412.

d Sirling, M. W. "Origin Myth of Acoma and Other Records," BBAAE, No. 135, Washington D.C., 1942. Quoted in Laura Makarius, "Ritual Clowns and Symbolic Behavior," *Diogenes,* Spr., 1970, #69, p. 47.

e Kallistos of Diokleia. "The Fool in Christ as Prophet and Apostle," in *Sobernost,* 1984.

f Zucker, W. M. "The Clown as the Lord of Disorder," in *Holy Laughter,* Hyers, New York, 1969, p. 84.

g Stephen, A. M. *Hopi Journal,* ed. Elsie Clews Parsons. New York: AMS Press, 1969, p. 554.

h Talayesva, D. C. *Sun Chief: The Autobiography of a Hopi Indian,* ed., Leo W. Simmons. New York: Yale, 1942, p. 109.

i Reeves, M. Journal, oral communication, Browning, Montana.

j *Akwasasne Notes.* Rooseveltown, New York, Spring 1987.

k Cushing, F. H. *Zuni Breadstuffs.* Museum of the American Indian: New York, 1975, p. 32.

l Beausobre, Iulia de. *Creative Suffering* (1990). Reissued as Fairacres Pub. 88 (Oxford, 1988), pp. 12–14, in *Kallistos,* p. 23.

m Sekaquaptewa, E. "One More Smile for a Hopi Clown," in *The South Corner of Time: Hopi, Navajo, Papago, Yaqui Tribal Literature,* ed. Larry Evers. Tucson: University of Arizona Press, 1980, p. 14.

n Cushing, pp. 620–22.

o Lame Deer, J. F. *Lamedeer, Seeker of Visions.* New York: Simon and Schuster, 1972, p. 225.

p Bateson, G. "The Position of Humor in Human Communication," in *Motivation in Humor,* ed. Jacob Levine. New York: Atherton Press, 1969. Quoted in *Hopi Ritual Clown: Life as it Should Not Be,* Louis Hieb, Ph.D., Dissertation, Princeton, 1972.

q Lame Deer, p. 229.

r Zucker, p. 80.

s Munitz, M. K. *Space, Time, Creation.* New York, 1957, p. 154.

t Hyers, p. 21.

u Hieb, p. 38.

v Witherspoon, G. *Language and Art in the Navajo Universe.* Ann Arbor: University of Michigan Press, 1977.

w Makarius pp. 45 and 64.

x Momaday, N. S. "The Native Voice" in *Columbia Literary History of the United States,* ed. Emory Elliott. New York: Columbia University Press, 1988, p. 7.

Normal

It is spring quarter, 1971. The early Carlos Castaneda books are in vogue. The religious studies department brings in a Hopi artist, a young man, let's call him Bill, to teach a course on Hopi religion. There are philosophy and religion majors, art students, a few Indians, the chairperson's wife, and some "townies" sitting in: maybe 35 eager people. On the second day Bill asks everyone to introduce themselves. When it comes his turn, a slightly unkempt man with his hair tied back into a knot and a multicolored headband says that he's lost his given name and family name while traveling in Asia. And since we are all a part of the oneness of the great universe, he's replaced it with the thousands of names of all the gods and goddesses in the Hindu pantheon. He then begins to softly recite these names: Atman . . . Brahama . . . Shiva . . . Vishnu . . . Kali . . . Krishna . . . on and on in a voice that belongs more and more to chant as each new name sounds from his lips. We wonder how long this young Hopi who is our teacher will permit this to go on and how he will stop it.

"OK. How about if we just call you Normal?" our teacher interrupts. This stops the flow of Hindu divinities from his mouth. He seems to accept this new name as his own. A literal wave of relief sweeps through the room. From that moment, for everyone, the slightly unkempt man with the blown-out look becomes Normal.

There are other incidents. Once Normal comes to class wearing an arrow prank on his head, the kind that looks like the arrow is shot right through your brain, but actually has a bend in it that goes up over the top of your head. Everyone pretends to ignore it, but that isn't easy what with Normal front and center with a joke arrow on his head listening intently to Bill lecture on Hopi religion. Another time, in response to one of Bill's questions to the class, Normal blurts, "It's these rubber bands we're wearing in our hair. They're interrupting the flow of blood to our brains. We've got to stop wearing these rubber bands." Bill seems to accept Normal without giving special attention to his antics, but the rest of us are uneasy, especially some of the Indian students.

It all peaks with the incident of the cushions. Normal has been absent for several sessions, after one in which Bill asked the non-Indians to leave so he could discuss aspects of Hopi religion that are esoteric, not for show. Everyone quietly filed out of the room except Normal, who refused to leave. None of us witnessed what followed, but rumor had it that when Bill tried to talk him into leaving, he insisted on his right to stay and listen, and there were angry words from some of the other students. It was even rumored that Normal pulled a knife, though no evidence of that ever came to light. However it went, Normal finally left and had not been back to class for a week or more. Meanwhile, the weather had warmed up and the class began to meet outside, sitting in a circle on the grass. Normal is a few minutes late on his first day back. He slips gingerly up to the circumference of the class circle and proceeds to get into the traditional yoga headstand posture right across from Bill. He remains in this posture for the full forty-five minutes remaining in the class. Pretending not to notice, we secretly fear he'll blow a blood vessel in his brain, but he walks off unimpaired at the end. Next session he arrives with two or three small cushions, one of which he sews on busily throughout the first part of class. At some point he breaks in on the discussion and says that he is making the cushions for the whole class, that we need them if we are going to sit on the ground instead of in chairs. But he needs help. If a few of us will offer to help him make cushions, in a day or two there will be enough for each of us. Then he gets up, walks across the circle and offers a cushion to one to the Indian students, as a token of peace, perhaps, for the touble he's caused. This man rejects it, tossing it into the center of the circle, saying he does not need a cushion to sit on the earth. The moment of silence that follows is intense. Bill gets up, walks over to the thrown cushion, saying, "Gee, I think I'd like to have one of these to sit on."

He picks it up and returns to his place where he sits on his new cushion, all as easily as if he were momentarily stretching and turning to look at a hummingbird or butterfly. From that moment Normal is a part of this temporary, fragile band of humans called a class, just as from an earlier moment he had simply accepted his original name from our teacher. Normal continues to sew quietly at his place in the circle for the rest of the term.

Transformation

SWEAT LODGE RITUAL NO. 1:
A BRIEF EXERCISE IN ETHNO-POETICS

PART I

one of the members of the [Omaha Pebble] society . . . was one day bathing, when he caught sight of a hawk, and fearing it was an enemy, he turned himself into a fish. The bird descended to get the fish, when the man eluded his fellow-magician by turning himself into a rock, and so escaped by his magic power, while his fellow magician, the bird, hurt his bill on the hard rock. There are many songs which refer to these magical transformations. (Fletcher and LaFlesche, p. 580)

One might question this account in the following way: Why didn't the Pebble Society member turn himself into a rock straight off, instead of first becoming a fish? Is it because he is bathing, is already part fish, when he first notices the hawk, immersed in that more ephemeral flow of air and sky? Or does the move first into fish trick the other magician into revealing himself — that wasn't just another hawk in the sky — and committing himself to the dive? Is timing what is important, then, the Pebble Society member changing into rock at the last possible instant, after attracting the other to him as a fish? Is turning oneself into rock the special province of Pebble Society members (literally, those who have the translucent pebble), from which other magicians are excluded? What might a person turn into in order to get at a rock? Fire? Larger rock to crush?

Without knowing if these are the right questions or whether questioning is the appropriate mode in which to approach this Omaha song, it does seem clear that what is called for is a suspension of the judgments emanating from our Occidental consciousness so that we may concentrate our attention, carefully and peripherally, on this magical movement of life from one form to another, across what we consider to be firm boundaries, and back again. For this power of transformation, this ability to "turn oneself into" some other form of life is central to the deepest experience of the Omaha, if we are to believe Fletcher and LaFlesche, and it informs in a significant way the work of the best Indian writers today. It also offers the promise of opening us up to the transforming powers of the natural world. What are the transformations we literally have traversed in our evolutionary journey from the so-called "lower" life-forms to ourselves?

Not unexpectedly, this transformative power is essential to the Omaha creation story as told by Wakidezhinga, the old leader of the Pebble Society, dead by the time Fletcher and LaFlesche published their work:

At the beginning all things were in the mind of Wakon'da. All creatures, including man, were spirits. They moved about in the space between the earth and the stars (the heavens). They were seeking a place where they could come into a bodily existence. They ascended to the sun, but the sun was not fitted for their abode. They went on to the moon and found that it also was not good for their home. Then they descended to the earth. They saw it was covered with water. They floated through the air to the north, the east, the south, and the west, and found no dry land. They were sorely grieved. Suddenly from the midst of the water uprose a great rock. It burst into flames and the waters floated into the air in clouds. Dry land appeared; the grasses and the trees grew. The hosts of spirits descended and became flesh and blood. They fed on the seeds of the grasses and the fruits of the trees, and the land vibrated with their expressions of joy and gratitude to Wakon'da, the maker of all things. (Fletcher and LaFlesche, pp. 570–71)

What is most striking about this old story is the sudden transformations that are integral to this place, this earth: rock appearing suddenly out of water, flames bursting forth from rock, water floating into air as clouds, grasses and trees appearing from earth. We, ourselves, partake along with "all things" of these sudden and powerful transformations in our origin, coming as spirits from the mind of Wakon'da to this place of water, rock, fire, and smoke-like clouds of steam. Eating changes seeds and fruit into flesh and blood, into bone. Grief calls forth primal rock from vast water. Joy makes the land vibrant and goes back to Wakon'da.

The sweat lodge of the Omaha Pebble Society is presented by Fletcher and LaFlesche as a formalized way to continue the expressions of joy and gratitude with which the land vibrated, and as the vehicle through which members of the society open channels of healing between these primal events, which are timeless, and those who are presently sick. Their account has attracted the attention of at least two Anglo poets, Jerome Rothenberg and William Brandon, who use it as the source for poems in English, Rothenberg giving us his "version" of the whole account while Brandon renders a poem about the "primal rock" of the first seventeen lines. If we apply the standard interpretive tools of the literary critic to the written account of this ancient ritual, we discover why it has attracted these modern poets: There is a living, rich quality to the imagery, the energy of first times and things and events has come into the language, and the human desire to be healed, made whole, is expressed with depth of longing and a promise of actuality.

PART II

Addressing ourselves initially to only the first part of the ritual, the source for Brandon's poem:

Free Translation of the Whole
1. He! Aged One, eçka
2. Thou Rock, eçka
3. Aged One, eçka
4. He! I have taught these little ones
5. They obey, eçka
6. Aged One, eçka
7. He!
8. He! Unmoved from time without end, verily
9. Thou sittest, eçka
10. In the midst of the various paths of the coming winds
11. In the midst of the winds thou sittest, eçka
12. Aged One, eçka
13. He! The small grasses grow about thee, eçka
14. Thou sittest as though making of them thy dwelling place, eçka
15. He! Verily thou sittest covered with the droppings of birds, eçka
16. Thy head decked with the downy feathers of the birds, eçka
17. Aged One, eçka
18. Thou who standest next in power, eçka
19. Thou who standest next in power, eçka
20. He! Thou water, eçka

21. Water that hast been flowing
22. From time unknown, eçka
23. He! Of you the little ones have taken
24. Though thy mysteries remain unrevealed
25. These little ones crave thy touch, eçka
26. He! Thou that standest as one dwelling place, eçka
27. Even as one dwelling place, eçka
28. Ye great animals, eçka
29. He! Who make for us the covering, eçka
30. These little ones, thou hast said, let their thoughts reverently dwell on me, eçka
31. He! Thou tent frame, eçka
32. Thou standest with bent back o'er us
33. With stooping shoulders, bending over us
34. Verily, thou standest
35. Thus my little ones shall speak of me, thou hast said
36. Brushing back the hair from thy forehead, eçka
37. The hair of thy head
38. The grass that grows about thee
39. Thy hairs are whitened, eçka
40. The hairs that grow upon thy head, eçka
41. O, the paths that the little ones shall take, eçka
42. Whichever way they may flee from danger, eçka
43. They shall escape. Their shoulders shall be bent with age as they walk
44. As they walk on the well-beaten path
45. Shading their brows now and again with their hands
46. As they walk in their old age, eçka
47. He! This is the desire of thy little ones, eçka
48. That of thy strength they shall partake, eçka
49. Therefore thy little ones desire to walk closely by thy side, eçka
50. Venerable One, eçka

(Fletcher and LaFlesche, pp. 571–73)

We find the earnest desire of the doctor, or shaman, expressed through two untranslated words, He! and eçka. He! is an exclamation involving the idea of supplication and distress. Eçka is a refrain meaning "I desire," "I crave," or "I implore." Actually, neither are translatable, according to Fletcher and LaFlesche. Eçka ends all but four of the 17 lines of this section (and all but 12 of the remaining 33 lines of the ritual). Of those lines not ending with eçka, only one of the first 17 is without the reverential exclamation "He!"; though 11 of the remaining 12 lines without eçka are also without He! This repetition of He! and eçka, plus the repetition of the phrase "Aged One," gives a decided chant quality to this part of the ritual, which lessens only slightly throughout. In Fletcher and LaFlesche's recording of the ritual in the original Omaha, the chant quality appears even more pronounced (see Appendix), the whole sound matrix of the first 17 lines made up, for the most part, of three repeated patterns and their variations. These chant qualities of the Omaha ritual are in no way excess baggage, but carry the intoning and imploring earnestness of the shaman on their shoulders as the meaning. He uses them to reenter the primal time of the ancient rock, of the sweat house, to open a healing channel of power to flow into these "little ones" (1. 4) who are sick. The most striking omission of Brandon's rendering

The Rock
(Fragment of a Ritual, Omaha)
unmoved
from time without
end
you rest
there in the midst of the paths
in the midst of the winds
you rest
covered with the droppings of birds

grass growing from your feet
your head decked with the down of birds
you rest
in the midst of the winds
you wait
Aged One
(Brandon, p. 83)

is "these little ones" who have been "taught" (prepared) by
the doctor, and who "obey." These are the sick people that the
Omaha doctor prepares himself to heal as he enters the sweat
lodge. The voice of the ritual is one of an intermediary: He
addresses the primal rock of their creation story, of the sweat-
house, directly, speaking of the readiness of the sick to receive
its healing power.

In Brandon's version, the timeless sense is retained, but not
the chant, and "rest" is used in place of "sittest" in describing
the rock, which, though less awkward in English, is also less
active, thus reducing the sense of the rock's life. In fact, in a
ritual for the sweat lodge before the initiation of a member of
the Pebble Society, the primal rock's act of sitting is made even
more explicit:

6. Oh! Aged One, eçka
7. The great water that lies impossible to traverse, eçka
8. Aged One, eçka
9. In the midst of the waters thou came and sat, eçka
10. Aged One, eçka
11. Thou of whom one may think, whence camest thou,
   eçka
12. Aged One, eçka
13. From midst the waters camest thou, and sat, eçka
14. It is said that thou sittest, crying: In! In! eçka

and

35. Oh! Aged One, eçka
36. Thou sittest as though looking for something, eçka
37. Thou sittest like one with wrinkled loins, eçka
38. Thou sittest like one with furrowed brow, eçka
39. Thou sittest like one with flabby arms, eçka
40. The little ones shall be as I am, whoever shall pray to
me properly, eçka

(Fletcher and LaFlesche, p. 577)

The "winds" of the Omaha ritual lose both their "various"
ness and their being "coming" winds in Brandon's working.
"Coming" especially seems indispensable because of its way
of centering the rock in the midst of winds coming to it along
various paths. And Brandon's version reverses the order of the
grass growing and the bird droppings and places the grasses at
the "feet" (his addition) of the rock (the Omaha ritual goes on
to associate the "small grasses" with the hair of the head, thus
extending a unified view of the rock as a being). The Omaha
ritual closes this opening section (ll. 13–17) by piling up the
details of the phenomenal world — grasses, droppings, feather
down — honoring the life of each in the naming.

Rothenberg's poem,

Sweat-House Ritual No. 1
Omaha

listen old man listen
you rock listen
old man listen
listen didn't i teach all their children
to follow me listen
listen
listen unmoving time-without-end listen
you old man sitting there listen
on the roads where all the winds come rushing

at the heart of the winds where you're sitting listen
old man listen
listen there's short grasses growing all over you listen
you're sitting there living inside them listen
listen i mean you're sitting there covered with birdshit
listen
head's rimmed wih soft feathers of birds listen
old man listen

you standing there next in command listen
listen you water listen
you water that keeps on flowing
from time out of mind listen
listen the children have fed off you
no one's come on your secret
the children go mad for your touch listen
listen you standing like somebody's house listen
just like somewhere to live listen
you great animals listen
listen you making a covering over us listen
saying let the thoughts of those children live with me
and let them love me listen
listen you tent-frame listen
you standing with back bent you over us
stooping your shoulders you bending over us
you really standing
you saying thus shall my little ones speak of me
you brushing the hair back from your forehead listen
the hair of your head
the grass growing over you
you with your hair turning white listen
the hair growing over your head listen
o you roads the children will be walking on listen
all the ways they'll run to be safe listen
they'll escape their shoulders bending with age where

they walk
walking where others have walked
their hands shading their brows
while they walk and are old listen
because they're wanting to share in your strength
listen
the children want to be close by your side listen
walking listen
be very old and listen.
(Rothenberg, pp. 280–81)

while keeping the chant repetitions of He! and eçka in his use
of "listen" nineteen times in his rendering of the first 16 lines,
loses some of the reverential tone of the original and moves
toward a more casual relationship to the rock in his use of
"listen" for He! and eçka, of "old man" for Aged One, and of
"birdshit" for "droppings of birds," though he's probably accurate in sensing that the Fletcher and LaFlesche rendering
was overly formal.

The second section of the ritual (ll. 18–25) addresses the
primal water out of which the rock rose as standing "next
in power" to the rock, as "flowing from time unknown."
The timeless "unmovedness" of the rock and the timeless
"flowing" of the water are set down together, both elemental
features of the world. Rothenberg renders "From time unknown" (l. 22) as "from time out of mind," and then the
"craving" of the little ones to touch the rock (l. 25) as "the
children go mad for your touch." This skew toward madness
and time being out of one's mind, I think, is a modern intru-
sion into the original, for pain and suffering (though they can
lead to madness) take many forms and usually are just that—
pain and craving for healing.

The shaman tells water, too, that the "little ones" (associated in their "littleness" with the "small grasses" of section

one?) have taken of it, though its mysteries "remain unrevealed," and they "crave thy touch" (ll. 23–25). This craving to touch and be near these elemental beings is central to the ritual. Also, the primordial rock and water "from time unknown" are literally present in the sweat lodge in the form of the heated rocks and the water that is to be splashed on them making steam (like the "waters that floated up into the air in clouds" when the primal rock burst into flames), and in the form of the water they have drunk.

In the third and shortest section of the ritual (ll. 26–30), the shaman directly addresses the sweat lodge and the "great animals" whose skins make the covering for it. It is addressed as "Thou that standest as one dwelling place, eçka," and this "as one dwelling place" is repeated, echoing the "dwelling place" of the rock amidst the small grasses of section one. "As one dwelling place," like the original land was one dwelling place for the spirits of all living creatures seeking to become flesh and blood, just as the sweat lodge itself is a dwelling place where spirits make their presence known. Perhaps it is the shape of the sweat lodge, too, humping up like a large rock, that adds to its association with the rock. In this one "dwelling place" of the sweat lodge, one realizes the deep interconnections among all aspects of life, not just rock, water, fire, and air, but the animals who've lent their skins, too and it is not only the "covering" of the sweat lodge that is evoked here, but the covering of the bodies of the Omaha with animal skins; in fact, an exchange of skins (and spirits) with animals is implied. The little ones are asked to think on this one dwelling place "reverently."

The fourth section of the ritual (ll. 31–46) opens by focusing on the willow frame of the lodge, explicitly including the plants in the "one dwelling place," though, to be sure, they have been present all along, as the "small grasses" of the primal rock, as the seeds of the grasses and fruits of the trees upon which the hosts of spirits fed when they first descended, and as the branches of trees and brush who gave themselves to be burnt to heat the rocks for the sweat. The frame of the sweat lodge, standing with bent back and stooping shoulders over the shaman (and, presumably over the little ones waiting to be healed) is the most powerful figure of the whole ritual, for the "little ones" are likened to this lodge person stooped with old age, thus their healing is treated as something that will occur:

> They shall escape. Their shoulders shall be bent
> *with age* as they walk
> as they walk on the well-beaten path
> Shading their brows now and again with their hands
> As they walk in their old age, eçka [emphasis added]
> (ll. 43–46)

"In their old age" just like the old age of the stooped one bending over them, just like the rock as the "aged one" from the ancient beginning.

The frame of the sweat lodge seems endowed with the quality of care for them (ll. 32–33), "bending over us" like a grandparent bending over a child, or as sky, too, oldest of grandfathers, arches over all. The willow frame of the lodge itself says, "Thus my little ones shall speak of me as 'bending over them with stooped shoulders.'" And this speaking of the frame of the lodge is accompanied by an act of care, as one might care for an old person:

> Brushing back the hair from thy forehead, eçka
> The hair of thy head
> The grass that grows about thee
> Thy hairs are whitened, eçka
> The hairs that grow upon thy head, eçka
> (ll. 36–40)

The little ones are urged by the lodge frame, through the ritual, to see it as bending over them, enclosing them in a healing way, and to actively respond by caring for it, brushing back the grass that grows about it, the grass that is its white hair. Through this act they themselves become stooped, white-haired, bending over others who will come to that aged care. It is the high point of the ritual, the "one dwelling" place where they may come to shelter in their sickness, and which echoes the dwelling place of the original rock among the "small grasses" where the spirits of all things came to dwell, and take on their fleshy bodies, and express their joy and gratitude.

Rothenberg omits the trees the grass is growing about (l. 38), thus weakening the explicit reference to the sweat lodge frame made from tree branches, and he also interprets the ambiguous "Brushing the hair back from thy forehead" as a self-act by the rock rather than as an act of the patients through which they engage the life of the rock and lodge itself in an act of caring — "you brushing the hair back from your forehead." He mutes the "desire" of the little ones, repeated twice in the last four lines, using the weaker word "want" only once, and misses the opportunity to connect the hands of the little ones "shading their brows" to "Brushing back the hair from thy forehead." His use of "children" for "little ones," though he explains in his commentaries that it is the patients who are being referred to, seems misleading. The slightly vaguer "little ones" allows us to experience our actual place in the world as frail and engaged with powers that dwarf us, but he ends as well, I think, as can be done in English,

> listen,
> the children want to be close by your side listen
> walking listen
> be very old and listen

The ritual itself ends with a section of four lines of great dignity and quietness, expressing the desire of the "little ones" to have this healing happen for them, "That of thy strength they shall partake, eçka" and expressing their desire "to walk closely by thy side, eçka/Venerable One, eçka."

The ritual is a circle, just as the lodge is, as earth is, as sky, ending with the strength of the primal rock which rose out of the waters and the desire of the sick people to walk close by its side. While we cannot presume to know what Omaha people might have experienced at this point, I imagine that if they did not receive the healing they longed for, the experience of walking closely by the side of the aged rock of "time unknown" would be affirming and sustaining even in illness and death. And perhaps entering the sweat lodge is the act of entering (going inside) the primal rock and primal time itself.

This identity of the sweat lodge and the primal rock of the closing sections of the ritual is made by the small grasses that the rock has for its "dwelling place" and that the "little ones" are to brush back from the forehead of the "one dwelling place" which the lodge is. It is made even more explicit in another section of the initiation ritual for the Pebble Society previously quoted: Here the primal rock and the willows that frame the lodge merge, for "Aged One" which has explicitly been the ancient rock for the first forty lines, becomes the willows as aged one.

41. Oh! Aged One, eçka
42. Oh! Thou pole of the tent, eçka
43. Along the banks of the streams, eçka
44. With head drooping over, there thou sittest, eçka
45. Thy topmost branches, eçka
46. Dipping again and again, verily into the water, eçka
47. Thou pole of the tent, eçka
(Fletcher and LaFlesche, pp. 577–58)

PART III

The point to be made is that the sweat lodge ritual from the Omaha Pebble Society is a clear expression of transformation as the primordial reality of the world (rock emerging from water, fire emerging from rock, water turned into clouds, etc.), and the shaman attempts to use this transforming power of the world to turn sick people into whole, healthy human beings, to use it to struggle against illness. The sweat lodge itself is a gathering place, not only of human beings, but also of their relations: gathering willow branches that make the skeleton of the lodge, the hides or blankets that provide the skin for it, the rocks that contain the heat of the heart sun stored inside the bodies of the trees that make the fire; gathering the water that changes into steam on the rocks, bathing the "little ones" in the dark heat, opening them to release the water that is deep inside, opening channels of life and pain and healing in the darkness, to be carried out of the belly of the lodge when the door is opened; gathering the darkness in which the sun's rock-water-fire may do its work; gathering sage, cedar, and sweet grass to purify the lodge and the dwellers in its belly; gathering songs and prayers, the joy and pain of the little ones of the lodge-belly; but gathering most of all the spirits of these, and of the old ones who come into the lodge to be happy, to heal. The lodge itself is a live thing, glowing, singing, gathering together the elemental universe with humans too, that they may acknowledge their true place in the world and ask for healing, for themselves and others — old people, rivers, the hunted. The sweat lodge gathers and vibrates with all that is gathered into it, much more than we know or know how to say. It is the primal rock of creation arising out of the vast waters in fire, fusing together the world in its gathering.

All this and much more is at issue in the sweat lodge, and

the poets feel it, though their retellings of it are a shadow of the Omaha ritual. That ritual resides in an intimate, living community, where people are sick and dying, and where certain specified, highly-trained members attempt to engage the creative powers of the world itself in order to heal. Our poetry, fine and powerful and necessary to healing our spirits as it is (and I am deeply committed to it), is removed from this. Unless we realize how much is lost in this movement from American Indian ritual into modern poetry, we will not recover the healing, transforming powers of the world of which we stand so much in need.

In closing, I'd like to quote a few lines from the Acoma poet, Simon Ortiz, in which this transformative power of the natural world is stated most intensely and beautifully in poetry that keeps faith with the old ritual experience, while still remaining poetry. They are from the long poem, "For Our Brothers Blue Jay, Gold Finch, Flicker, Squirrel," from the first section, for Blue Jay. Note the power of Blue Jay's wing to turn the sun itself into "actually black" and to flash the purest light from that black sun, though this is a remembered power as Ortiz is confronted with a dead blue jay:

> O goddammit, I thought,
> just lying there.
> Thought of the way he looks,
> swooping in a mighty big hurry,
> gliding off a fence pole
> into a field of tall dry grass,
> the summer sunlight catching
> a blade of wing, flashing
> the bluegreen blackness,
> the sun actually black, turning
> into the purest flash of light.
> (Ortiz, pp. 128–31)

Ritual for Sweat Lodge, No. 1

1. He! Inshage' eçka
2. In'e shninke she eçka
3. Inshage' eçka
4. He! zhinga' wi ewe'ponçe thonde
5. Egon bi eçka
6. Inshage' eçka
7. He!
8. He! gthin a'biton thethe xti
9. Thagthin' adon eçka
10. Tade' ui'the the'non ha te thoneçka
11. Tade' baçon egon thagthin' adon, eçka
12. Inshage' eçka
13. He! xa'de zhinga thon thon eçka
14. Uti'e'thathe egon thagthin' adon eçka
15. He! wazhin'ga a'zhazha xti thagthin' adon eçka
16. Hinxpe' a'gthagtha xti thagthin' adon eçka
17. Inshage' eçka
18. Edi uwa'ton eçka
19. Edi uwa'ton eçka
20. He! ni nike she eçka
21. Ni nike aton adi'ton
22. Gaçu'çe shnin e inte eçka
23. He! du'ba thi'thiça i te
24. Utha thithin'ge te thonzha eçka
25. Zhinga' i'thite gon'tha i te thonzha eçka
26. He! Ti thaton she eçka
27. Ti thaton she eçka
28. Wani'ta tonga eçka
29. He! itha' kigthaxade eçka
30. Zhinga' ui'the ungi'kaxe ta i te eshe ama thon eçka
31. He! tishi thaton she eçka

32. Non'xahi thiba'gizhe xti
33. A'baku thiba'zhu thon
34. Nont'u'ça xti
35. Zhinga the uithe ungikaxe ta i te thonzha eçka
36. He! pehin'bixa'xadon eçka
37. Nonzhi'ha thon the'thon
38. Xa'de thon hin a'zhi adon eçka
39. Hinthon çka don eçka
40. Hin a'zhi te thon e'waka i don eçka
41. He! monthin ta i ke eçka
42. Win'unwata uki'mongthon i ke eçka
43. A'baku thon nont'u'ça xti
44. Uzhon'ge nonçta xti i ke
45. Pe a'çon githe ihe'thatha xti
46. Monshnin' adon Inshage' eçka
47. He! zhinga' gikon'tha badon eçka
48. Ithigikon'tha tabadon eçka
49. Thie i'wigipathin ta mike thonzha eçka
50. Insha'ge eçka

Here is a contemporary poem that seems worthy of association with this old Omaha ritual.

Stone

Go inside a stone.
That would be my way.
Let somebody else become a dove
Or gnash with a tiger's tooth.
I am happy to be a stone.

From the outside the stone is a riddle:
No one knows how to answer it.
Yet within, it must be cool and quiet
Even though a cow steps on it full weight,

Even though a child throws it in a river;
The stone sinks, slow, unperturbed
To the river bottom
Where the fishes come to knock on it
And listen.

I have seen sparks fly out
When two stones are rubbed,
So perhaps it is not dark inside after all;
Perhaps there is a moon shining
From somewhere, as though behind a hill —
Just enough light to make out
The strange writings, the star-charts
On the inner walls
(Simic, p. 59)

Columbus Day Revisited

AMERICAN INDIAN LITERATURE &
HISTORICAL/LINGUISTIC TRUTH

The failure of institutions of so-called higher education to integrate into their curricula the information and point of view originating in the native cultures of this land leaves us, as a society, grossly ignorant of where we actually are, of the true history of our coming here, and of such essentials as the meaning of our own language, not to mention the issue of intellectual honesty. I do not mean to reduce the significance of the need for women's studies, black studies, Asian studies, or Hispanic studies. Obviously, much the same things could be said about the failure to integrate these elements of our history/society into our educational systems. But I do wish to suggest that the native peoples of this Turtle North Island America have a special and compelling claim in our history, our psyche, and our prospects for the future. The nature of that claim has to do with their deep rootedness in this land (and by land I mean much more than merely the soil—land includes all the waters, minerals, winds, insects, plants, fishes, birds, reptiles, animals; all the forms of life through which the land expresses itself).

Native peoples are the people of the land—the land itself

speaks through them in several ways: in its ability to renew itself, in the magical capacity for transformation from one life-form to another, in the felt-pain at the holocaust visited upon the land by an invading industry/state/economy. Their literatures, both oral and now written, contain the best hope we have of coming to our senses, which means regaining our self-respect and interdependence, our respect for all the other forms of life with which our own fate is bound up, for our own tenure on the land is superficial, though deeply scarring, in comparison.

Listen to this statement by Oren Lyons, Onondaga traditionalist from the Iroquois nation, about his uncle teaching him who he is, his identity with and from their particular land:

> I was fishing with my uncle, he's an old chief from home and we were out there in a boat in the middle of the lake and talking about this and that. I had just graduated from college at that point, you know, and I was kind of feeling my oats a little bit.
>
> And we were talking and he said, "My, you are pretty smart, you know. You learned a lot of things." I said, "Yeah." I was surprised and he said, "Good, then you ought to know who you are then." "Sure," I said, "I am Farlan Lyon." He said, "Yeah, that's who you are, I guess. Is that all?" So I started to suspect right away something is going on here. Here I am in a boat and I can't get out and we're out in the middle of the water and he said, "That's your name all right. We know that. Is that all you are?" Well, I started thinking. I started to feel a little track already and I went to my father's line, my mother's line, my clan. I searched and he chased me all over that boat for two hours. He wouldn't let me out. I was ready to swim. I was

getting mad. Then I said, "Well, who the hell am I then?"
And he said, "Well, I think you know, but I will tell you.

"If you sit right here and look over there, look at that. The
rocks. The way they are. The trees and hills all around you.
Right where you're on it's water!" And he said, "You're just
like that rock." And I listened. He said, "You're the same as
the water, this water." I waited and listened again, as he
said, "You are the ridge, that ridge. You were here in the beginning. You're as strong as they are. As long as you believe
in that," he said, "that's who you are. That's your mother
and that's you. Don't forget." I never have. (Lyons, p. 11)

It seems to me that it's the forgetting here that marks the
difference between Anglo and Indian cultures in relation to
the land. Not to know the land, particularly and intimately, is
to leave oneself open—open to the machinations of the market, so-called culture.

The second point I want to make has to do with Indian
history. Their historical perspective gives us a vantage point
on our own history that is essential. "History is written by the
victors." Knowing this axion places upon us a terrific responsibility to try to uncover, often through a record that is frag-
mentary and consciously twisted, the fullest possible history
of which we are capable.

This brings me to Columbus, the 500th anniversary of
whose "discovery" of America we are celebrating in 1992.
Columbus thought he was in India, hence his name for the
inhabitants—Indians. Or was it that he thought they were
extremely close to the creator because of the harmony of their
lives and so called them In Deo—in with god, as Russell
Means suggests? Where do we think we are? How can we tell
where we are? Who can give us the answers? Who are the na-
tives? What do they know about this place? What grows here?

In 1988, I accepted an invitation to be scholar in residence for the Arizona Humanities Council at the largest Indian high school in the U.S. — on the Navajo Reservation: 1,400 students; 95 percent Navajo, three percent Hopi, two percent Ute, Havasupai, Crow, Anglo. My charge was to infuse the humanities into the curriculum, with special emphasis on Navajo and Hopi culture. As part of my fulfillment of that charge, I relied on the poetry written by young Indians in the last twenty to twenty-five years. The voice of beauty, pain, and power raised in this poetry is astonishing; is, as I've said, the voice of the land itself. During the year, five Indian poets came into the school to read and teach, and a poem by an American Indian was published each Friday in the school bulletin, which was read second hour in all classes. The administration was extremely sensitive about what poems appeared in the bulletin — I had to clear my choice each week with the principal, a Navajo, supportive of the project but unpopular with his faculty and fearful of being accused of being racist if the Friday poems were too hard-hitting. The students had been fed a steady diet of Anglo standards — *Beowulf,* Shakespeare, Wordsworth — and most had little sense of either their own literature or history.

At a meeting with the school English Department over the issue of including more Native American literature in the curriculum, we had teachers who said openly that to bring in the Native literature was an attempt to take us all back to the cave. "We all started in caves!" was the comment. And when asked about the environmental wisdom contained in that literature, we were told: "We don't need it. When we ruin this planet, we'll get into our spaceships and go to another, and when we ruin that one, we'll go to another, and when we ruin that one, we'll go to another, and another, and another. That's what technology is for." This person, whose father was reported to be a teacher of Shakespeare at a Canadian university, not only actually believed this, he taught it to young

Navajos to prepare them for entry into the white world. How many like him come through our existing schools to become teachers? How might exposure to Native traditions in literature begin to dissolve that hard-heart knot of the religion of high-tech escape from the consequences of our actions on planet Earth?

Second semester, in order to make it possible to include a wider range of poems in the Friday bulletin, I began to attend the weekly chairpersons' meetings — to read and discuss with them the poem that was to appear that Friday. This was a group of twenty or so people, mixed male/female, Anglo/Navajo/Hopi. At my third or fourth session with them, I chose to work with Jimmie Durham's Columbus Day.

Columbus Day
In school I was taught the names
Columbus, Cortez and Pizzaro and
A dozen other filthy murderers.

[At this point, the white Chair of the physical education department, a fundamentalist, married to a Navajo, jumped up and down in his chair and blurted out, "I protest, I protest." I read over the top of his protest.]

A bloodline all the way to General Miles,
Daniel Boone and General Eisenhower.
No one mentioned the names
Of even a few of the victims
But don't you remember Chaske, whose spine
Was crushed so quickly by Mr. Pizzaro's boot?
What words did he cry into the dust?

What was the familiar name
Of that young girl who danced so gracefully
That everyone in the village sang with her —

Before Cortez' sword hacked off her arms
As she protested the burning of her sweetheart?

That young man's name was Many Deeds,
And he had been a leader of a band of fighters
Called the Redstick Hummingbirds, who slowed
The march of Cortez' army with only a few
Spears and stones which now lay still
In the mountains and remember.

Greenrock Woman was the name
Of that old lady who walked right up
And spat in Columbus's face. We
Must remember that, and remember
Laughing Otter the Taino, who tried to stop
Columbus and who was taken away as a slave.
We never saw him again.

In school I learned of heroic discoveries
Made by liars and crooks. The courage
Of millions of sweet and true people
Was not commemorated.

Let us then declare a holiday
For ourselves, and make a parade that begins
With Columbus's victims and continues
Even to our grandchildren who will be named
In their honor.
Because isn't it true that even the summer
Grass here in this land whispers those names?

And every creek has accepted the responsibility
Of singing those names? And nothing can stop
The wind from howling those names around
The corners of the school.

Why else would the birds sing
So much sweeter here than in other lands?
(Durham, pp. 10–11)

At the close of the reading, the "physical education" chair
began to explain his protest. He thought the poem presented
things from the past that were too negative, that were best
forgotten, and what we needed to do for our students was give
them positive experiences. They already had enough negatives
in their lives. A short discussion occurred both as to whether
or not the poem was negative and as to what the students
needed from us as educators. One of the Navajo chairs said —
We've got three students here to make a presentation; why not
ask them what they think? We did, and one, a young woman,
a junior, spoke for all three. "Of course there are things in our
history as Indian people that are dark and very painful. There
are parts of our history that are difficult to know and to accept. But we students can endure our own history; we need to
know it; we can accept it because it's the truth. And that's our
main need from you, our teachers — we need to hear the truth,
no matter how hard it is."

That ended the discussion. She spoke so well, so concisely.
"Columbus Day" was in the bulletin on Friday. I come back to
this incident often in my mind. It has a classical structure to
it — a young Navajo woman, sixteen years old, instructing
twenty department chairs plus the principal, plus the humanities scholar on the preeminence of the truth of their history —
their hunger and need to know who they are (for their identity
and self-esteem) — and knowing that Jimmie Durham, Cher-
okee, gives them some information on the "discovery" of
America that they haven't (and probably won't) find in history
textbooks or at Columbus Day celebrations.

How accurate is Jimmie Durham? What are his sources of
information? Why isn't this information more widely known
and taught? And if Navajo kids in Arizona need to know the

truth of their history, Anglo kids in Bellingham, Washington or Chilicothe, Ohio need it just as much, for their identity and so that the ongoing holocaust perpetuated against all forms of life on this planet that has been accelerating for centuries may be slowed and its energy redirected rather than intensified. One hopes that the Native perspective on Columbus will be prominent in the coming celebrations of this 500th anniversary.

Near the beginning of this essay, I stated that we don't even know the meaning of our own language, let alone the truth of our history. What do I mean? I'm stunned when I actually crack open certain words that I've taken for granted ever since I learned them, to discover that inside are ancient, crystal-like seeds that no one in my hearing or reading has even implied were there, and that constitute layers of richness in the word, in the language, that simply are absent in both the use of the words and in the intellectual discussions about language and meaning to which I am privy. This happens often enough that I no longer take for granted that I know the meanings of even the most common words in American English; the experience of having particular words crack open like this, revealing ignored, hidden seed crystals, is exhilarating and a little disconcerting. I've found that the study of Native literature intensifies this sensitivity to language, to understanding just what words mean. This is so, I think, because through this literature, even in translation, we come into contact with other languages, other meanings, and then are driven back onto our own — to be clearer about just what we have meant all along, about just what is being carried in our language. History and language intersect there, for it becomes clear to us that those parts of our own history that are buried and forgotten are implicit in the oldest, forgotten meanings of our words.

The young woman who stood by her need for the truth of her history stays with me. I retell her story frequently. After one such retelling back in Montana, I realized that I didn't know the meaning of that simple word true. This drove me back to Webster's; let me retrace for you my etymological path. True — akin to Greek treu; Indo European base, derew — a tree (see tree), basic sense, "firm as a tree." Here it was again — an abstract word, true, leading straight back to a concrete word, tree, and to a specific attribute of tree — firmness, rootedness. No one had ever suggested in my hearing that the truth had anything to do with trees. I thought of the clearcuts in Montana; of the bodies of those trees sunk in the harbors of Japan; of the two hundred acres of virgin oak my great-great-grandfather had burned in Ohio to make his farm; I thought of the barren, rocky slopes of Greece denuded to build the Athenian fleets; I thought of the rain forest, cut and burned to raise beef for hamburgers; I thought of the Siberian tiaga, about to take the next massive hit from corporate logging; I thought of Gary Snyder's Wasco Indian logger who sold his chain saw and apprenticed himself to a medicine man because he couldn't stand to hear the trees scream as he cut into them; I thought of the truth of trees — Tree — akin to Gothic triu; IE. base, derew, a tree, see dryad. Dryad: Greek, dryas, drys, an oak, tree, see druid: in Greek mythology, any nymph (or goddess or female spirit living in a tree). And so there it was — the word true having some strange origin in the female spirits living in trees in the earliest layers of memory in our own language heritage. And the word druid, yes, or dru-wid as the IE. base signifies, meaning, literally "oak wise," from the same base as tree and true, derew; the spiritual leaders of pre-Christian, Celtic Europe — their wisdom explicitly linked to the female spirits living in trees, to the truth contained there. Dru-wid — oak wise — tree wise — truth wise — tree, wise female tree. No wonder one of the first things the Roman legions did when occupying the lands of Celtic peoples they wished to dominate was to cut down and burn the ancient, sacred groves of oaks, like Spaniards burning Mayan histories, oaks within which lived the female spirits of nature. (Was my great-great-grandfather in Ohio simply carrying on this old Roman tactic?) And no wonder that Robin Hood's mythic resistance to a later invader emanated outward from the ancient oaks of Sherwood Forest. I thought of the great totem spirits emerging from the carved bodies of cedar trees all along this Pacific coast northward. I thought of tribal people in India tying themselves to trees in an effort to save their forests and soils; I thought of young people sitting for days in old larch and fir and pine trees in Montana in order to protest or stop old-growth timber sales; I thought of the rivers of mud swallowing thousands of people after the recent rains in the Philippines. I felt as if my very own tradition were a magical thing, containing wisdom and knowldge of which one might be proud. But I wondered why no one had taught me my own tradition!

Native Americans know this truth of the female spirits residing in trees and have not broken with these spirits. And they know that other, allied truth — the historical/ecological terrorism emanating from those societies who have lost their memories of the interconnections to land, to plants, which Oren Lyons's story warns against. To forget that what's true emanates from things such as trees is to turn a reduced version of the truth into yet another weapon of the domination of everything. But, on the brighter side of this true/trees link — Black Elk tells us that the cottonwood tree leaf — its shape — is the origin of the idea for the tepee, a correspondence of forms. And that the cottonwood tree sends the most prayers to Skan/ Sky, oldest of grandfathers, because its leaves move in the slightest breeze. These and many other reasons are why the cottonwood tree is the center pole at the sun dance.

Seven years ago, I had the opportunity to witness a sun dance on the Rosebud Reservation. Perhaps two hundred of us stood around the medium-sized cottonwood at its place in the forest as the religious leaders prayed to/with it, made offerings to it, with a young woman, a maiden. And then, each of those who had vowed to dance the sun were given, in turn, the ceremonial axe and took four strokes with it into the body of the tree, until finally the tree was severed. And eventually all two hundred people literally carried the whole body of the tree together, singing the two miles back to the Sun Dance ground. More ceremony was done there, including placing buffalo fat in the purified hole that had been dug to receive the butt end of the tree—buffalo fat to feed it, to keep it strong. And before it was hoisted, all present were invited to tie into its upper branches their prayers—tobacco offerings wrapped in colored cloth—red, blue, yellow, green, white, purple—so that when the tree was hoisted, all its branches fluttered with the brightly colored prayers of the people.

The religious leaders spoke about the importance of the tree for the Lakota, as it was about to be raised: "We need the tree to pray for us; because of its innocence, an innocence we cannot recover, its prayers are pure and can get through to the Creator. So tie your prayer bundles onto the branches of the tree and let it pray for you." And in the afternoons, the people would line up to give offerings of their flesh to be tied in small cloth bundles and offered to the tree—flesh prayers.

After four days of dancing, song, fasting, prayer—days in which young men had literally hung up in the tree from thongs placed through their breasts, their arms flapping like wings in rhythm with two hundred eagle-bone whistles, blood pumping in jets from their open breasts, the Sun Dance ground was quiet. Most people had gone home. A small boy lay in the crotch of the tree, like in a nest, daydreaming. The whole place hummed with the power of this ancient solar generator. I watched small wind-tears appear in the beautiful "Free Leonard Peltier" banner stretched over the east gate to the Sun Dance ground, and commented to a friend: "Look, that banner is starting to tear." "Yes," he said. "Next year at this time there'll be just a few scraps of cloth from it still tied to those poles. The rest will have gone on the wind to Skan, in the form of prayers for Leonard." "Yes," I answered, glad I had not spoken the rest of my mind—that we should take it down, fold it up, and store it away for safekeeping. The banner was like the leaves of the tree—and not to be separated from those processes of wind and weather that are the true way power moves in the earth. Tree-truth.

The best reason, perhaps, to integrate into the curriculum American Indian literature, as well, I think, as women's studies, black studies, and Asian studies, beyond the alternative perspectives and the revision of our history so as to make our society more just (no small matters), is that studying Native traditions reawakens us to that in our own traditions which is/was native—to the female spirit residing in trees that is a truth, an origin of truth, without which we may very well ruin this beautiful planet (and without spaceships to carry us to another). The forging of such cross-cultural links is among the most important businesses we now have, for in that process, we discover in ourselves what we thought resided only in others.

Navajo High School
I
No one in this school — 1400 Navajos —
has heard, revolt against the Spaniards
from Taos to every Pueblo.
Men run with the new moon,
carry the secret
as far as the Hopi villages.
The Franciscans burn
sixteen hundred kachinas,
more than forty Pueblo priests
flogged in the plaza in Santa Fe.
No one has heard,
though the track team wins state
and the only Indian in English,
Rex Lee Jim, runs right off the pages of the book.

Here it is strictly Anglo,
how to raise your child.

The English head,
the "Highest-paid teacher in the state of Arizona,"
says in the Phoenix paper,
"The old ways and their culture
are as much in their minds as cancer,"
and objects when a teacher shows a film
on Wounded Knee, 1890 —
"We don't want to upset the kids."

The kids, in response
to a questionnaire,
"What Indian ways mean to me":
1. No Indian way for me, I don't know it, so I'm going
   science.
2. Get rich the fast way.
3. Don't know, don't care.
4. Kill the whites, yet not be traditional.
5. To be traditional — be poor and on general assistance,
   live off the government and
   commodities.
6. Boonies, food stamps, mutton, collect feathers.
7. Sorry, don't know.
8. Staggering and pass out — crazy and puts shame
   to your name.
9. Speak Navajo or die.
10. Wipe out the whites and live free as long as the
    grass grows.
11. We're practically gone and I hate that.
12. Be an Indian but don't look or act Indian.
13. Indian way of life is just superstitions.
14. I'd rather keep it to myself.
15. Sorry, don't know.

II
I urge English
to include Indian lit in their courses.
"What about progress?
We all started in caves," one teacher blurts.
"But there's environmental wisdom in these
traditions."
"We don't need it.
When we ruin this planet
we'll get in our spaceships and go to another,
and when we ruin that one
we'll go to another
and to another and another and another.
That's what technology is for."
(At a year-end party
he leaps into his Cessna
and flies to the nearest off-reservation
liquor store when the booze runs low —
that's what technology is for.)

III
An old woman, no English,
is brought into the classroom
before her next presentation.
After the lecture
she talks with one of the students.
"She wants to know if she can make a speech too."
She stands very straight,
speaks softly but formally,
with great dignity.
He translates:
"She says when she grew up around here there were no
stores, and hardly any fences —
just the trading post, hogans, and some government
housing.

Little streams of water used to trickle
like webs over the ground.
The little streams of water are gone now
and the white man is here,
so get an education
so you can talk the white man's language
and get a good job."
She sits in the back of the room.
"Could you ask her to tell us a story?"
One of the hoods, in the back too.

The translator speaks with her,
then silence.
"What's the matter?"
"I can't ask her," he says.
"Why not?"
"I don't know the word for story," he says,
deeply embarrassed.
"Do any of you know the word for story,
how to ask her to tell us a story?"
More silence.
We sit a small eternity
together in this pain,
panic flitting
the edge of my paralysis;
for them, humiliation
in front of their elder,
for her, I would not deem to guess.

IV
We read *Navajo Stories of the Long Walk*,
accounts of pregnant women shot by soldiers
because they couldn't keep up,
of elders dying of dysentery from the alkali
water at Fort Sumner,

or of soup made from green coffee beans
tearing their guts out.
They cannot contain their anger,
anger piled up three, four generations.
A silent, slight student who doesn't need the credit
turns in only this:

> *I never knew so much hate could one person have as*
> *when I read about pregnant women getting killed*
> *because they could not walk anymore. I think the only*
> *really big thing that happened to me was that my*
> *emotions could not handle all the sorrow and it turned*
> *to anger. Only when it turned to anger did I relieve*
> *myself of this terrible burden. I killed a crow at one*
> *hundred yards with the wind blowing in gusts. It was*
> *an almost impossible shot. But one bullet was all I*
> *needed that day. I was surprised to see my bullet find its*
> *mark as the crow slid down into the ravine where it*
> *was standing.*

Barbicito surrenders to the army near Tuba,
goes to Fort Sumner
to renew the mind of the people.
Barbicito,
putting the white shell bead
in the mouth of coyote,
the abalone shell of their flesh
into coyote's mouth —
to find a way between the crashing rocks.

V
Late in the year
Felipe brings the deer dancers in,
Yaquis from Marana
with their raspers, water drum,
and tenevoim, the butterfly cocoon rattles
tied to the dancer's legs,

to sing and dance the deer for us.
The last night
he asks everyone
to come down
and take some water from the drum,
for a blessing for ourselves, our families.
Everyone stands in line like communion,
to touch the water that now contains
the songs and dances of the deer,
the end of drought.

Later, the students say,
"We thought those Yaquis were just Mexicans
pretending to be Indians
in order to get government benefits.
But now we see they're just like us Navajos.
Those Yaquis are a spiritual people."

VI
Teaching poems at the chairperson's meeting,
the one about the child
transformed into a bear
and how the bear priests call him back again,
the head of phys ed blurts,
"You expect us to believe that?"
"I expect you to believe
whatever you want.
But know that this child's
transformation
into a bear
is one of the oldest,
widest spread stories in the world—
believe what you want."

Reading Jimmy Durham's Columbus Day—

"In school I was taught the names
Columbus, Cortez, and Pizzaro and
a dozen other filthy murderers,"
he protests again:
"The students don't need that.
They have too many negatives in their lives already.
Our responsibility
is to give positive images,
not to dig up old hurts."
A woman student answers —
"Yes, there are parts of our history
that are painful, that hurt.
Of course it is difficult
to learn these things.
But we can endure that pain
because they are the truth.
That's all we need to hear from our teachers,
the truth."

KGAK radio in Gallup
finds a medicine bundle in the street,
announces it over the air —
no one claims it.
They store it four years,
then give it to Navajo Community College:
a medicine bundle from the streets of Gallup,
10 of 26 ceremonies
from the turn of the century
now extinct.

VII
Every Wednesday at eight a.m.
James takes us to the hogan
for culture class,
songs and Navajo tea.

He sings the song
to make the mountains come alive again.

This will come and be —
this will give direction to mankind,
this which will come and be —
this placed within the dawn. . . .
the first words that earth speaks.

And corn pollen will erase the bad things
we say and think and do,
corn pollen mixed with ground turquoise on the tongue.
You can use the dust of the earth,
earth's pollen,
if you don't have the pollen of corn.

James sings the song:

Take only a small amount of soil from each
mountain,
the amount scooped up
on a small arrowhead
at a certain place in the song.

The faces of the students become
the faces of children again.
They clutch the mountain-soil bundle close,
the first time in their lives.
James sings the song
to make the mountains come alive again.
If you don't have corn pollen
use the dust of the earth.

A weaver comes to class.
Her rugs go to Smithsonian.

"Do you leave the 'mistake,'
the spirit line, in the rug
so the evil spirits can get out?"
one of the students asks.
"Dooda! No.
No evil spirits."
"What's it for, then,
the 'mistake' in the rug?"
"It's because you can't be perfect.
To acknowledge that in your weaving.
To say it in beauty —
you can't be perfect.
That's what it's for."

VIII
Almost at the end
there is a ceremony
to bless the school.
James translates for the old man —
"The hogan is our law.
When the Navajos were placed on this earth
and the earth could still speak,
she proclaimed that we were her children.
That is why we call her mother earth . . ."
Each one goes to him and prays with the corn pollen,
sprinkling it gently into the cloth
he has spread upon the ground.
When all have prayed
he wraps together the prayers sprinkled into the cloth.
He will take them to a beautiful place,
watch over them four days.
When it is finished
he blesses James with pollen.
"Believe now,
and go do your work,"

ancient eyes alive and smiling
behind thick glasses.

IX

    Let there be beauty before you,
    Let there be beauty behind you,
    Let there be beauty beneath you,
    Let there be beauty above you,
    Let there be beauty around you,
    Let there be beauty within you.
    You are the children of beauty.

The chants,
they unwrap the evil and sickness from around us.
It's because we can't be perfect.
To say that in beauty.
He sings the song to make the mountains come alive.
And all our faces become the faces of children again.

Works Cited

Armstrong, V.I. *I Have Spoken*. Chicago: Swallow, 1971.

Babcock, Barbara. "Arrange Me into Disorder." In John Mac-Aloon, ed., *Rite, Drama, Festival, Spectacles: Rehearsals Toward a Theory of Cultural Performance*. ISHI Press, 1984.

Basho, M. *The Narrow Road to the Deep North and Other Travel Sketches*. Baltimore: Penguin, 1966.

Brandon, W. *The Magic World*. New York: William Morrow, 1971.

Brown, W. *Oral communication*. Butte, Montana.

Bugbee, H. *The Inward Morning*. State College, Bald Eagle, 1958.

Deloria, V., Jr. *God is Red*. New York: Laurel, 1973.

DeMallie, R.J. *The Sixth Grandfather, Black Elk's Teachings Given to John G. Neihardt*. Lincoln & London: University of Nebraska, 1984.

Durham, J. *Columbus Day*. Minneapolis: West End Press, 1983.

Eckhart, M. *Meister Eckhart: A Modern Translation*, Raymond B. Blakney, tr. New York: Harper & Row, 1941.

Evers, L., ed. *The South Corner of Time*. Tucson: University of Arizona Press, 1983.

Fletcher, A.C., and LaFlesche, F. *The Omaha Tribe*. Lincoln: University of Nebraska, 1972.

Gleick, J. *Chaos, Making a New Science*. New York: Viking, 1987.

Goethe. *Faust,* Louis MacNiece, tr. New York: Oxford University Press, 1951.

Hart, J.A. *Montana — Native Plants and Early Peoples*. Helena: Montana Historical Society, 1976.

Heidegger, M. *Poetry, Language, Thought*. New York: Harper & Row, 1971.

Hilbert, V., ed. and tr. *Haboo: Native American Stories from Puget Sound*. Seattle: University of Washington Press, 1985.

Humphrey, S. K. *The Indian Dispossessed*. Boston: Houghton, Mifflin, 1905.

Josephy, A. M. *The Nez Perce Indians and the Opening of the Northwest*. New Haven: Yale University Press, 1965.

Kaiser, R. *"Chief Seattle's Speech(es): American Origins and European Receptions,"* in Arnold Krupat, ed., and Brian Swann's *Recovering the Word, Essays on Native American Literature*. Berkeley: University of California Press, 1987.

Lee, D. *Freedom and Culture*. New York: Prentice Hall, 1959.

Lyons, O. Quoted in *"America as Holy Land,"* Peter Nabakov, *North Dakota Quarterly*. Autumn, 1980.

Mathews, C. *The Elements of Celtic Tradition*. New York: Barnes & Noble, 1989.

McNickle, D. *Wind from an Enemy Sky*. San Francisco: Harper & Row, 1978; repr. University of New Mexico Press, 1988.

Momaday, N. S. *"The Native Voice,"* in *Colombia Literary*

History of the United States, ed. Emory Elliott. New York: Columbia University Press, 1988, p. 7.

—— *The Way to Rainy Mountain.* Albuquerque: University of New Mexico Press, 1969.

Neihardt, J. G. *Black Elk Speaks.* Lincoln: University of Nebraska, 1961.

Ortiz, S. J. *A Good Journey.* Tucson: University of Arizona Press, 1977.

Parsons, E. C. *American Indian Life.* Lincoln: University of Nebraska Press, 1922.

—— *Isleta, New Mexico.* Annual Reports of Bureau of American Ethnology, Vol. 47. Washington D.C.: Government Printing Office, 1931.

Rasmussen, K. *Intellectual Culture of the Iglulik Eskimos.* Copenhagen: Gyldendalske Boghandel, Nordisk Forlag, 1929.

Reeves, M. *Class journal* (used with permission). Missoula: University of Montana, c. 1975.

Rothenberg, J. *Shaking the Pumpkin.* Garden City: Doubleday, 1972; repr. University of New Mexico Press, 1991.

Sembene, O. *God's Bits of Wood,* Frances Price, tr. Garden City: Doubleday, 1962.

Silko, L. M. *Ceremony.* New York: New American Library, 1977.

Simic, C. *Dismantling The Silence.* New York: George Braziller, 1971.

Snyder, G. *Earth House Hold.* New York: New Directions, 1969.

Stevens, W. *Collected Poems.* New York: Knopf, 1954.

Swanton, J. Quoted by Gary Snyder in *Proceedings of the Right to Remain Wild, a Public Choice.* Missoula: University of Montana, 1975.

Turner, F. W., III. Introduction to *Geronimo: His Own Sory.* S. M. Barnett, ed. New York: Dutton, 1970.

Tyler, H. A. *Pueblo Birds and Myths*. Norman: University of Oklahoma Press, 1979.

Van der Post, L. *A Bar of Shadow*. New York: William Morrow, 1956.

—— *The Heart of the Hunter*. New York: Morrow Publishers, 1961.

White, L.A. *The A'coma Indians, People of the Sky City*. Glorieta, NM: Rio Grande Press, 1973.